Roadmap to
RESPONSIBILITY

The Power of *Give 'em Five*™
to Transform Families

LARRY THOMPSON
MELISSA BECK AND ANGELA THOMPSON

Cover design, book design and layout by Jim L. Friesen

Library of Congress Control Number: 2017961515

International Standard Book Number: 978-0-9963253-2-5

Dedication

This book is dedicated to our parents. They have always been in our corner and were willing to live and work through life together—in the good times and the hard times. Losing our father, and father-in-law, has made us aware of the influence our parents have throughout our entire lives. He had a tremendous impact on so many lives, and we want our children to remember his influence on our family. For all of us, our legacy lives on in our children and in future generations. May this book serve to make your influence and your legacy all you would wish it to be— now and always.

Table of Contents

Introduction

When setting out on a journey, we have a clear destination in mind. From the start, we are headed somewhere in particular. We watch for road signs. We ask, "Are we on the right track? Have we missed a turn? Is this the correct exit?"

The parenting journey is filled with decisions. Which concerns are most important? How do we handle all these endless scenarios? Every child is different. Every age and stage brings a new set of complexities. In addition to the challenges of life in general, parenting adds additional twists and turns to the journey.

The purpose of this book is not to instill guilt or regret. As you read, you will identify areas of strengths as well as areas where you may struggle or desire to grow. None of us, including the authors of this book, claim to parent perfectly. Forgive yourself for mistakes and pull out your new map, load the kids in the car, and begin a new journey.

Responsibility-Centered Parenting™ (RCP) will help you identify your destination and recognize when you are getting off course. Your destination will be kept in sight, and you will be able to stay motivated to keep moving in the right direction.

On this adventurous road of parenting there are three different styles that parents tend to use:

- Permissive parents are strong in warmth and acceptance, but make few demands. They just want their children to be happy. They are strong in emotional support, but may be uncomfortable holding the line when children push back against the limits. For these parents' leadership may be weak, and expectations may be low.
- Rules and control are high priorities for authoritarian parents. Warmth and acceptance are contingent on performance. These parents are strong on issues of consistency and clear expectations, but often try to control others by utilizing strong, negative emotions. Their children may not feel supported in coming up with their own solutions. The result can be high levels of tension in the family and low levels of connection and shared joy.
- Authoritative parents—those using *Responsibility-Centered Parenting*—can blend together warmth and acceptance, while still challenging their children to grow in maturity. These parents do not veer off the road to either side—left or right. They are balanced as they provide genuine warmth and clear, consistent expectations.

The concepts in this book are the tools you will need to put this balanced parenting style into action. We will define the common exits parents create for their children off the Road to Responsibility—that path that will lead children to becoming mature, responsible adults.

With time and training, you will be able to recognize when and how you may be making it easy for your children to escape solving their problems and, therefore, lose the opportunity for them to grow in independence.

When parents and children can stay together on the Road to Responsibility, children are required to think critically. With emotional support from their parents, they will— maybe for the first time—tap into their own creativity to solve their problems. As they develop this skill, they will learn that they can handle life as it unfolds. By the time they launch into full independence, they will have an internal resource that has been practiced many times.

Responsibility-Centered Discipline™

Whenever we are invited to speak in schools and at national conferences, we are always asked, "Do you have a book on parenting?" While attendees are listening to a presentation on school discipline and learning how it has changed lives in school systems across the country, their thoughts, naturally, turn to their own families.

The stories, which inspire them and move them to tears, also produce a momentary vulnerability. They ache to see their own children and grandchildren succeed in life and remain "on the Road to Responsibility."

Now, Responsibility-Centered Parenting is here, offering renewed hope for families.

Regardless of culture, income level, or family makeup, when it comes to the children in their lives, parents long for positive, lasting solutions.

What sets RCP apart from most frameworks for families is that it does not rely on the two go-to strategies normally utilized: reward (tokens) and punishment (consequences). Instead, RCP—like its counterpart RCD—teaches responsibility, rather than dispensing tokens for good behavior or consequences for bad behavior.

Can responsibility be taught? This is a question we continue to be asked, and the answer is still, "Yes!"

Many parents either discipline their children in the same way they were raised or in opposition to it. Regardless of which method is employed, tokens and consequences seldom produce internalized standards of behavior. Yet, parents may think their strategies are working if they see *external* compliance. But those externals are short-term occurrences versus a life-long development of *internal* character.

My wife, Angela, and I created Responsibility-Centered Discipline well over a decade ago, while I was working in a very difficult alternative school setting. The concepts, which were first implemented in that school, are now common practice in schools in all fifty states, Canada, and parts of Europe.

Although RCD was developed for schools, it became clear that the principles were just as applicable in other sectors and arenas of life: work, marriage, parenting — basically, anywhere people interact with people.

As you read this book, you will begin to understand how many of our traditional ways of doing things actually move us away from promoting responsibility.

Responsibility-Centered Parenting (RCP)

RCP is not a new way of *doing*, but it is a new way of *thinking*.

Angela, my sister (Melissa), and I have been in discussion about this book for years. Melissa's work as a family therapist and her firsthand familiarity with the development of RCD and RCP, have made her the perfect colleague for this collaboration.

I want to take a moment to thank my wife. Angela and

I have coached each other through the hard moments with our kids. I have not only watched her be a wonderful mother, but I have watched her be an amazing stepparent as well.

I also want to thank Melissa for sharing her expertise, wisdom, and insights as a professional and as a parent. Her family is a beautiful example of what happens when parents are balanced in what she describes as demandingness and responsiveness. She and her husband have modeled RCP and raised three wonderful children who are growing into mature, responsible adults.

If you read my first book, *Roadmap to Responsibility: The Power of Give 'em Five to Transform Schools*, you are familiar with Melissa already from this story I shared:

I was always a strong-willed child. I would weigh my options but end up doing what I wanted to do. Whenever my parents warned me of a consequence for disobedience, I would think it through: "Is this action worth that consequence?" For me, sometimes it was.

Our family was traveling by car from Kansas to California, back before seat belts were the law. I was a rambunctious child, so I am sure I was making the trip a challenge, especially for my two sisters. My dad kept telling me to sit down, be still, and keep quiet. Finally, after many warnings, he said, "If I have to tell you again to sit down, I'm going to pull the car over and spank you right out on the side of the highway."

Well, I did not heed his advice, and I did end up getting the spanking. As we pulled back onto the highway, my two older sisters were smiling and enjoying the moment. Teary-eyed, I looked at one of them and whispered, so my dad couldn't hear me, "I may be sitting down on the outside, but

I'm still standing up on the inside."

That memory is an important one for me when I think about our discipline methods. Do we want children to obey on the outside without growing in responsibility internally? If they are "still standing up on the inside," can we expect to see the growth of character that will benefit them for a lifetime?

We want children to grow in maturity and responsibility, not to comply based on external force. Using the Roadmap to Responsibility™ means giving children the time and tools necessary to increase their critical thinking skills, improve their confidence, and enhance their ability to solve their own problems.

I'm sure Melissa has her own stories to tell, too. Thankfully, we not only grew up as siblings, but we also grew up to be friends and colleagues. I am profoundly grateful for the time, patience, and passion she has invested in this book. Our hope is that it will help you and your family members grow as individuals as well as grow closer together.

Larry Thompson

PLEASE NOTE: *Names and identifying details have been changed to maintain privacy. All stories and scenarios are intended to communicate general principles and relational dynamics.*

Chapter 1
Roadmap to Responsibility

As parents, we know the frustration of trying to get our children to behave. We want the best for them. We probably want it more than they want it for themselves. Yet, there are so many days when parents feel they are banging their heads against a wall.

The more they talk, the less their children listen. The more they try, the angrier or more emotional they get, and the less their children appear to care. Parents want to save their children from all the trouble that could come with irresponsibility.

You start with a simple, immediate goal—a non-emotional assignment such as, "Make your bed." Day after day, you try to get your child to follow through. You try rewards. It works for a time, but then it stops working. You try consequences. It works for a time, but then you grow tired of having to follow through on the consequences. Soon, you realize you are putting more work into it than it would take to make the bed yourself. You fall into that trap for a while, until you decide to try a new reward system—and the cycle begins again.

1

When your child asks, "Why do I have to make my bed?" you try very hard not to say, "Because, I said so, and I'm your parent. That's why!" Your deepest frustration is not about an unmade bed. It is because you know this type of irresponsibility grows with the child. Today, it is the bed, tomorrow, the car. And, before too long, this child will be grown and gone. You say, "Make your bed!" but the real worry is, "If I can't get you to do one simple thing, how am I going to get you safely through the teen years?" And, most importantly, "Who will you grow up to be if you don't develop the internal strength to take responsibility for yourself, your choices, and your life?"

Staying on the Road to Responsibility

Typically, parents do not plan to drive left across the median into oncoming traffic or veer right off the road into a ditch. Yet, we have all probably inched out of our own lane and needed to pull back on the wheel to avoid an accident. We all know that uh-oh feeling of dread as well as the feeling of relief when we are back in our own lane.

Fortunately for drivers, most roads provide telltale reminders when motorists move off the road and into trouble. Bumps between lanes, concrete barriers, and shoulders provide boundaries. When we veer too far off the road and our tires meet the rough shoulder, it makes a distinct noise— giving us the heads-up that we are passing the boundary line and moving into harm's way.

Responsibility-Centered Parenting provides the boundaries and barriers parents need to keep their children on the Road to Responsibility.

Not Knowing *What* to Do Is Stressful

We know what it feels like to try our best and still feel like we are failing. Often, the biggest frustration is *not knowing what to do*. Over time, this stress can affect our outlook, emotions, and even our health.

What we know about the brain is that a stress-driven, fight-flight-or-freeze response may help in a survival situation, but it is not a healthy long-term strategy. The chemicals released when we are under pressure, and the wear and tear on our bodies due to prolonged times of stress, are extremely unhealthy.

A stress-ridden environment diminishes learning and personal growth. "Whenever there is a perceived threat, the brain's ability to think, plan, problem-solve, and control impulses is inhibited or shut down. Learning becomes more difficult or impossible," says Dr. Spencer Kagan in his book, *Brain-Friendly Teaching*, (Kagan Publishing, 2014). Therefore, we never want to use tactics that inhibit or shut down our own or our children's ability to think, plan, problem-solve, and control impulses. We want to do the opposite.

Unfortunately, many parenting techniques elevate stress. In contrast, when our thinking changes from pushing and prodding our children to guiding them to take responsibility, we can calm ourselves and recognize the teachable moments all around us. Using RCP, we can turn these moments into opportunities for personal growth and better outcomes for the whole family.

If We Want Different Results, We Must Learn New Skills

Parenting is full of challenges, but RCP provides a way to develop new skills to use, even in the most challenging moments. When learning how to parent under pressure, a classic example to follow is the job of a paramedic. Paramedics come on the scene of an accident and, rather than react based on the severity of the situation, they go right into their trained responses. They might be thinking, "Wow, this is bad," but because they have learned what to do through thorough training, they push those thoughts down and begin to act out of experience, not emotion. If a paramedic can learn to respond based on his or her skills and training in life-and-death situations, I am confident parents can be trained to respond in a productive way, even when things get difficult.

{ Because we know the parent-child relationship is one of the most important in a child's life, and we know that relationships are more at risk when emotions escalate, then learning how to parent in a way that strengthens the relationship, rather than damaging it, is one of the most valuable skills we can acquire. }

How It Began:
Larry's Story

Throughout the book, we will share stories to illustrate Responsibility-Centered Discipline and, more specifically, Responsibility-Centered Parenting.

After working with the same students over and over as a school principal, I became very frustrated. Even though I used the techniques I was taught in college and teacher training,

I saw little to no change in students' attitudes or behaviors.

It felt as though the methods of discipline led to one big revolving door. Giving students consequences for their actions was easy, but they always ended up back in the same place—the principal's office.

This is how Responsibility-Centered Discipline™ and the Roadmap to Responsibility™ were developed. Rather than making short-term, external compliance the objective, my goal was to consider what was in children's long-term best interest.

At least one positive thing came out of the revolving-door approach to discipline. I heard the same responses from different students, over and over. Using an analogy of a road, I recognized that these responses represented common "exits" students would try and take to avoid responsibility. The words might vary, but the exits were the same.

I also discovered that this process is the same at home as it is at school or at work.

As parents, some of the common excuses we hear from our children to exit the Road to Responsibility will sound something like this: "Mom, you let us do it yesterday, and you didn't say anything." (Consistency exit); "No one told me." (Clear Expectations exit); "If you're going to yell at me, why am I in trouble for yelling back?" (Emotional Control exit). These are three of the six common exits children use that we will cover in more detail later.

I realized that recognizing these exits, and knowing what to say and do in challenging moments, could keep difficult situations from escalating. This helps create a home environment where parents are more confident and less stressed and where children are kept on the Road to Responsibility.

Teacher and Mom:
Angela's Story

When I first met my husband, Larry, he had a one-and-a-half-year-old daughter, London, from his first marriage. I remember observing him as he interacted with her. I could see what an incredible father he was. This was one of the many things that made me fall in love with him. I quickly grew to love his sweet, energetic daughter also. I learned so much from my husband about parenting even before we were married and had children.

As an elementary school teacher, I began to implement this same philosophy and these same strategies in my classroom. I experienced such a positive change, not only in my students, but also in myself. I was no longer stressed and frustrated with behaviors in my classroom. As both a teacher and a mom, what I learned about RCD and RCP has helped me view challenging behaviors with my students, and with my own children, as opportunities for teaching and growth.

RCP Encourages Healthy Independence:
Melissa's Story

Many of life's lessons come unexpectedly. We may not recognize how profoundly the experience impacts our lives. Aubrey's story is a good illustration of why it is not in our children's best interest to try and solve their problems, even when things get tough.

When we arrived at Taekwondo class, all the parents were abuzz with awful news. Aubrey, our children's six-year-old classmate, had been in an accident, and her right leg had been amputated. We all wondered how the family would cope.

Many months passed before Aubrey returned to class using her new prosthetic leg. Her parents sat near me, watching as Aubrey bent down to remove her prosthetic leg before heading to the water fountain. Her parents smiled, explaining, "She says it slows her down." Aubrey proceeded to hop on one leg to the other side of the room to get a drink. She couldn't reach the fountain, so she hopped over to a step stool, hopped back to the fountain carrying the stool, maneuvered herself up onto the stool, and took a big drink. Then, she hopped off the stool, put it back in its place, and headed back across the room to class—all with a smile on her face.

To my astonishment, Aubrey's parents were relaxed as we watched the entire process together. They did not jump up to help her. They did not anguish over her challenge or appear to feel the need to comment. They did not inject themselves into the situation in any way. These parents displayed complete confidence in their daughter's ability to accomplish her goal. They sat at ease, visiting with the other parents as normally as they had prior to the accident. I am sure Aubrey knew they were available to her if she needed them, but they let her lead.

That winter, I received an email from the family with a picture of Aubrey on snow skis, smiling from ear to ear. A note said she was planning to train for the Para-Olympics in downhill skiing. She had a coach and was working her way up the ranks.

Looking Down the Road to Responsibility

Most parents want the same things for their children. We want our children to grow to be good people who can be trusted, have a strong work ethic, and make positive contributions to the world. We want them to be successful and independent and to reach their full potential.

None of us brings a baby home from the hospital with the intent of having the child become a disrespectful, irresponsible, or lazy adult. Most parents want their children to feel safe and loved and grow to be well-adjusted, successful adults.

So, how do we create a family atmosphere where children can develop the internal strength and skills needed to direct their own lives in a positive and lasting way? How do we help them gain the capacity to self-motivate, regulate emotions, and have self-discipline, without having them become self-centered?

In this age of technology, social media, and the degradation of family culture, this challenge has become even more difficult. Therefore, a clear Roadmap to Responsibility is required.

Traditionally, parents have used tokens and consequences (reward and punishment) and the element of time to persuade or pressure their children into external obedience. But do these methods work? It depends on the goal.

What's the Goal?

Is our goal to make our children comply in the short term or is it to keep them on the Road to Responsibility and guide them to internalized values in the long term? Unless we are willing to address this tough question, we may send our children mixed messages that have profound and unanticipated consequences. In doing so, we allow them to exit the Road to Responsibility.

In contrast, Responsibility-Centered Parenting focuses on the long-term goal of character development, not short-term tokens such as getting an A or winning a game.

We should ask ourselves:

- What are the real goals we have for our children?
- What do our children perceive our goals to be?
- Are these goals the same?
- Is external obedience or internal character more important to us?
- What value have we placed on providing warmth and acceptance?
- Are we requiring character development for our children?
- Do we expect more of our children as they mature?

Before You Begin

Responsibility-Centered Parenting is filled with powerful concepts that will help you maneuver the twists and turns of parenting. As you learn more, you will become better equipped to handle the challenging moments all parents face.

You will learn more about how to keep your family safely on the Road to Responsibility.

Like driving a car, we cannot control the road conditions, but we can make sure everyone in the car is wearing a seatbelt. We cannot control how other people drive, but we can remain alert and react and respond accordingly. In other words, there are things we can control and things we cannot.

Similarly, we cannot control how other people behave, but we can create a calm, comfortable, and safe atmosphere in our homes rather than a stressful, chaotic environment.

Chapter 2
Self-Control

If we neglect to provide children with Clear Expectations, Consistency, and Leadership in Challenging Moments or if we lose our Emotional Control—relying on consequences and withdrawing support through challenging moments—we are placing our children in harm's way.

Tokens and Consequences

Because it is difficult to stay on course on the Road to Responsibility, parents may veer left (permissive) or right (authoritarian). Parents veering right tend to rely more on negative consequences and withdrawal of support. Parents veering left tend to use tokens, rewards, negotiation, and bribery to get children to behave. They also can be too lenient and inconsistent in their parenting.

"If you're good, I'll buy you a toy."

"If you get an A on your test, we will go get ice cream."

"If you clean your room, then I'll get you a new outfit for the party."

When we reward children with tokens, they just want more tokens to do the things they should be doing anyway. Tokens can cause children to develop a *bottomless pit* or

11

black hole syndrome. They cannot get enough "things" that they do not need. Over time, they only feel happy if there is a material reward at the end. They lose the ability to experience the internal satisfaction that comes from hard work and persistence.

Never Withhold Affection to Motivate Children

Parents who veer right rely more on negative consequences and withdrawal of support. But when we withhold our praise or affection in an attempt to motivate children, it can cause the unintended consequences that breed a lack of confidence and insecurity. A parent's anger does not motivate. It may intimidate or manipulate the child into obedience, but it will be external compliance, not an internal change in thinking or behavior that will last long term.

Of course, it is a good thing when children care about how their parents think and feel, but that should not be their motivation for doing their best. Our hope is that our children will develop their own passion and drive to be successful. More importantly, we want them to consider character and "giving your best effort" as the goal. Doing the right thing should be most important versus becoming an A-student or a top athlete.

People only change their behavior, permanently and internally, when they are ready and willing to change. They change when they feel a need to change. They change when they see the personal benefits to them. Change will not be permanent if children are only trying to adhere to someone else's rules or demands.

Relying on consequences, rewards, shame, withholding love, or anything else that "solves" the problem, other than the child, limits the child's development of self-control.

Overcorrecting

While trying to find a parenting strategy that works—to get their children "to obey"—some parents will overcorrect and go too far the other way.

For example, Susan and Jim divorced when their children were young. Susan had custody of the children most of the time. The oldest, Joshua, was starting to push the limits. For two weekends in a row, he had missed his curfew by fifteen minutes. He told Susan that he and his friend were playing football, and he lost his keys in the grass. Once he found them, it was already past his curfew.

Veering Left

Mom: "You should have called me."

Joshua: "Mom, it's not a big deal. Most of my friends were still out. I was the first one that had to leave. You make everything such a big deal. I've been out after curfew before, and you didn't say anything. Why are you getting so upset this time? It's not like I'm doing anything wrong. I was with Thomas. You know he's not going to get into trouble. If you're going to nag me all the time, I'll just stay at Dad's on the weekends. He doesn't care when I come in."

Mom (feeling guilt): "I know you're not out getting into trouble. Just, please, try to be home by midnight next time."

Susan feels bad for Joshua and his siblings. She knows the divorce has made life difficult, so she tries to make up for it by going easy on them. She thinks, "Why make life harder?"

Besides, she really hates it when Joshua talks about staying more with his dad, and he knows it.

Veering Right

Susan: "I've had it with you, Joshua. You're late, again. That's it. Give me the keys. You can just walk or ride your bike if you want to go somewhere. And you can take the bus to school, but you're going to follow my rules! There's no excuse for your behavior. If you keep this up, you can just go live with your dad. Let's see how he likes being disrespected all the time."

Joshua: "Mom, it's not a big deal. Most of my friends were still out. I was the first one that had to leave. You make everything a big deal. I've been out after curfew before, and you didn't say anything. Why are you getting so upset this time? It's not like I'm doing anything wrong. I was with Thomas. You know he's not going to get into trouble. If you're going to nag me all the time, I'll just stay at Dad's on the weekends. He doesn't care when I come in."

Mom: "I'll talk to your dad tomorrow, but be ready to pack up your stuff, because I can't handle you anymore."

Joshua: "Perfect. I'm glad to leave. It's like a prison in this house. You're always checking up on me. None of my friends have to deal with this stuff. They just go home whenever they want to."

Susan: "You have a thousand excuses, don't you, Joshua? But the bottom line is you were late. What's going to happen when you have a job? Are you going to get to work late and give the boss a bunch of excuses? How are you going to keep a job acting like that?"

Joshua storms out. Susan is left feeling angry and hurt,

dreading the regret she knows she will experience as soon as her anger dissipates.

Responsibility-Centered Parenting

The centerpiece of RCP is Give 'em Five—an interpersonal communication framework used in every challenging discipline scenario. This is the tool used to keep children on the Road to Responsibility or to lead them back onto the road when they have exited.

The five components of a Give 'em Five conversation are:

- Support – Supportive comments given to and for the child
- Expectation – Clear expectations shared beforehand
- Breakdown – The Breakdown of those expectations, identified and shared with the child
- Benefit – Short- and long-term Benefits to the child, if he or she adheres to expectations
- Closure – Closure in the conversation, acknowledging next steps

We will learn more about Give 'em Five in Chapter 11. Here is an example of how it would be used in the above scenario.

Susan: "Joshua, this is becoming a problem. When you were late last weekend, I let it slide, because you are usually good about your curfew (Support), but now that it's happened again, we should talk (Breakdown). Being home by midnight requires you to keep track of the time and plan ahead (Expectation). When you're home by midnight, you have use of the car when you need it. I want to trust you to have the freedom to come and go as you need to. Knowing I can trust you about curfew shows me I can count on you in other areas as well, so you get more opportunities to go do things you want to do (Benefit). I'm going to ask for the keys while you figure out a plan to help you make your curfew, even if there's a problem like losing your keys. Let me know when you're ready to talk about your plan, and we'll get this figured out" (Closure).

Temptation is all around our children, especially in the teen years. Our teens must develop enough self-control to resist the temptations such as missing curfew, drinking, using drugs, and engaging in sexual activity. Self-control is just that: self … control. Joshua is learning this through the Give 'em Five conversation. His mom has closed every exit off the Road to Responsibility. She requires him to let go of the many reasons for missing his curfew and solve his problem. This builds Joshua's self-control as he learns to stop and think versus react and walk away.

Developing Self-Control

Jill snuck into her older brother's room and borrowed his phone without asking. In the past, she had asked Aiden to borrow it, and he had given her permission. This time, she skipped a step.

Aiden wasn't home, so she thought: "He won't mind."

When Aiden returned after school, and his phone was not where he left it, he shouted furiously, "Jill, where's my phone?"

Mom to Jill: "We all have things that are important to us, and your brother's phone is important to him. You've been good about asking him if you could borrow it (Support) and

16

because of that, he usually lets you, (Benefit) but it breaks trust when we take other people's things without their permission (Breakdown). Asking him first lets him know you respect him and that he can trust you (Expectation/Benefit). Please return the phone to Aiden, and think about how you will prove to him that he can trust you in the future (Closure)."

Children who grow up practicing self-control are more likely to maintain jobs, earn promotions, and develop healthy relationships with others. At the same time, the relationship that individuals have with "themselves"—one of self-control and empowerment—is one of the most important relationships there is because it is the foundation upon which all others are built.

As our children learn to talk to themselves in a supportive way, it helps them establish thoughts and attitudes that affect their actions. Teaching children how to think about *how* they think gives them skills to slow down their processing and respond rather than react to their circumstances. This process of solving their own problems develops an internal habit. As they learn to talk to themselves in a positive way, their attitudes and actions are impacted. When we support their problem-solving with curiosity by asking questions such as: "How did you do that? What worked for you last time? Is there a way you could try that again?"—this causes them to *think* about *how* they think.

Helping Children Regulate Their Emotions

Little League games are a great place for observing parenting styles and children's levels of Emotional Control. Whenever a bad call is made by the umpires, some children will get angry and yell, "That's not fair!" Others will break down and cry in frustration. A few will say something like, "Come on, team, we can do this!"

Children show a wide range of responses to strong feelings. Children who can learn to understand and control their own emotions will better understand how others feel. In contrast, children who regularly lose emotional control will have trouble making and keeping friends; and children who withdraw from emotional challenges will be less likely to try new things.

> Teaching children how to regulate their emotions gives them a skill they will use for the rest of their lives.

Things to keep in mind while helping children grow in self-control:

- Remember that training the brain to stay in control improves with practice and maturity.
- Know that consistency gives a young brain a sense of stability and predictability.
- Validate strong emotions before addressing them. Example: "I see you are very angry."
- Share your own emotions of frustration, sadness, and fear appropriately. Example: "I feel disappointed, too, that your team didn't win."
- "Name it to tame it" was coined by Dr. Dan Siegel. Helping children identify the emotion by naming it helps them process and tame the emotion.
- Model emotional control.
- Ask questions: "What can you say to yourself that could help you when you feel angry, sad, or left out?"

- Plan ahead whenever there is the potential of an emotional explosion (big game, hard test, etc.), and use these as learning opportunities for your child to grow in self-control rather than rescuing them ("Here's a prize, anyway.") or lashing out at them ("So, you lost! Big deal! Get over it!").
- Provide children with external structures such as routines and chores.

The ability to self-regulate and exercise responsibility is empowering. When we blame other people for our behavior and make excuses, we allow others to "rule us." We become emotionally limited rather than growing more confident and independent. When we can say, "I have control over my choices," it places us in a position of power. It enables us to change our circumstances or, at least, to impact them more positively.

RESPONSIBILITY

RESPONSE -ABILITY

LEADERSHIP IN CHALLENGING MOMENTS

CONSISTENCY

CLEAR EXPECTATIONS

EMOTIONAL CONTROL

BENEFITS FOR CHANGING BEHAVIOR

Chapter 3:
Parenting Styles and Exits Off the Road to Responsibility

Around the age of eighteen to nineteen months, toddlers begin wanting to comply with their parents' demands. How parents react and interact with their children when they are young is highly influential on their development. When parenting, a positive demeanor and a reliance on negotiation rather than direct control correlate with higher compliance in toddlers. In research by Dr. Cheryl Marsiglia, a positive parenting style has been linked to the development of a healthy self-conscience.

Based on that research, positive self-esteem in childhood was also associated with positive mental health later in life, and a lack of self-esteem has been related to social dysfunctions and mental pathologies, such as depression and anxiety. Overly high self-esteem issues, based on unrealistic expectations, also have been found to correlate with dysfunction in peer relations. For example, excessive praise without parents providing boundaries may result in a child developing narcissism.

Positive Self-esteem

Self-esteem develops when we know we are loved and valued. It does not develop from excessive praise. Children brought up to believe they are special or exceptional may grow up to have a positive self-esteem, however, an indulgence of praise and attention may cause them to have an unrealistic assessment of themselves.

When parents shower children with praise, they may have an inaccurate measurement of their talents and abilities. They think they are exceptional. This unrealistic evaluation of their skills sets them up for failure and disappointment. They usually blame their failures on factors outside of themselves. The reasons they are not recognized or promoted are confusing to them. They are not prepared for the demands of a boss and the complexity of adult relationships. They expect special treatment.

We want our children to have positive self-esteem as well as a realistic evaluation of their skills.

Participation in activities like dance, sports teams, and learning a musical instrument teach character. Few children will reach the professional levels in these areas, but that should not be the main goal. Far more importantly, they can learn things like:

- Persistence
- How to lose gracefully
- How to stay humble in victory
- How to be happy for others when they succeed

When Responsibility-Centered parents offer praise, the focus is on the child's character growth and internal processes. "You brought your grade up from a C to a B. How did you do that? That takes a commitment and determination. I'll bet you feel good about yourself. I'm proud of you, too."

When we praise the growth process, our children will pay more attention to their own character than they will to external prizes and recognition. When they want to quit, they are able to say to themselves, "I'm not giving up just because it's hard or because I didn't place first." Rather, they can feel good about themselves because they did the right thing. They stuck with boring, mundane, time-consuming practice or rehearsals and gave their full effort to reach a goal. Responsibility-Centered parents notice growth in character more than who won the game or came in first.

Parenting that promotes healthy self-esteem involves:

• Accepting children, so they feel safe and valued
• Setting clearly-defined limits for behavior
• Allowing individual expression
• Respecting unique personalities and points of view

Permissive

The primary goal for parents when they veer left is a desire to eliminate, or at least minimize, their child's experience of negative emotions. These parents are highly responsive, but they require little of their children. As their children mature, the parents are most concerned with not upsetting their child. They find it very difficult to hold a position of leadership until the child solves the problem. These parents do what they can to keep the peace. When their child is unhappy, frustrated, disappointed, or angry, parents veer left and over-identify with the child's feelings. They want the child's bad feelings to stop. The discomfort the parents feel when their child struggles makes it difficult to set healthy limits, because setting limits causes the child to express negative emotions.

Such parents negotiate, threaten, and count to three (*ten times*). They explain their reasoning and do just about anything to get the child to be okay with the request. The longer children go without demands being placed on them, the more difficult it is to shift them to something new. Obviously, a teenager who has been allowed to manipulate her parents most of her life, with pouting, yelling, withholding her love, or throwing a fit, will not be able to transition quickly or smoothly into taking responsibility and solving her own problems.

{ Before we can integrate Responsibility-Centered Parenting into our families, we must be realistic about our current parenting style. Good questions to ask are: "How was I parented?" and "Is that the model I want to use with my children?" }

Permissive or Authoritarian Versus RCP

Again, the three parenting styles people tend to use are:

- Permissive (veering left) - Lax and inconsistent
- Authoritarian (veering right) - Rigid and controlling
- Authoritative (RCP) - Balanced and flexible

Parents drifting left on the Road to Responsibility tend to rescue children from solving their own problems. Parents drifting right on the Road to Responsibility tend to heap on more and more consequences, thinking this will motivate children to change. Parents using RCP follow a balanced approach.

'This bed is TOO soft!'

As it was with Goldilocks, we are all looking for the right fit. Whether it is a bed-or a balanced parenting style, we want something that works and feels right. Parents moving left are like a bed that's too soft—comfy at first, but not in one's best interest long term. Children's emotional outbursts can throw the entire family into anxiety. The child's strong display of emotions is given too much power and weight.

Being permissive tends to result in having inconsistent boundaries and a hard time setting limits. In a family where the parents drift left, it is difficult to know who is in charge—the parents or the children. In these families, sometimes children end up having to "parent" younger siblings or children are given too much power, confusing the leadership role of the parents. The parents may lack the skill of leading in challenging moments.

Children may be left unsupervised for longer periods of time than appropriate. Children who grow up in chaotic environments often feel more anxiety and insecurity. Because we know safety and security are foundational for maturation and growth, veering left off the Road to Responsibility is counterproductive to the goals we have for our children.

'This bed is TOO hard!'

Parents moving right are like a bed that's too hard. They have such rigid boundaries. Their children learn to follow rules, but they do not learn how to make good decisions on their own. They may become susceptible to others with stronger minds and wills. As they grow up, they can become inclined toward depression and anxiety. Pushing back respectfully against authority is not an option in some veering-right families—even when those in charge are abusive. Questioning authority is viewed as a threat in such a setting. Thinking is shut down and children will do about anything to ensure they are not emotionally abandoned. They will internalize negative emotions and play it safe.

In some cases, children's loyalty to the family system causes them to feel guilty for wanting to have their own opinions. Often, they are punished for separating from the family's hidden rules. One unspoken rule may be, "We will accept you, if you do not become your own separate person." Guilt and manipulation can continue into adulthood. Sometimes, a child who has grown up in a veering-right family will marry someone with a strong will because, subconsciously, he thinks: "I do not have the strength to buck the system, so I will attach myself to someone who can do it for me." In some cases, the children of parents drifting right off the Road to Responsibility may not learn to think for themselves because someone else has made many of their decisions for them.

Emotionally enmeshed (overly-connected) families perceive individuality as a threat. They discourage separation. In the end, children are torn between becoming a separate self or holding on to the love and acceptance of their family.

Veering-right parents may be motivated by fear or use fear as a motivator. They constrain independent thinking and feeling. The family becomes one big, enmeshed unit. To feel loved and accepted, children learn not to explore their own ideas and feelings but, instead, they fall in line with what is emotionally safe.

"This bed is JUST right!"

As a parenting tool, RCP is just right. Parents moving left and right both curtail or suppress moral reasoning development as well as a child's personal internalization of standards. Children may show external compliance while being observed, but this is not the same as being a responsible individual.

According to research by M.C. Boyes, professor of psychology at the University of Calgary, a balanced parenting style produces the highest level of moral reasoning. In contrast, parents veering right produce the lowest level of moral reasoning.

Using Responsibility-Centered Parenting, we stay centered. We keep our children on the Road to Responsibility because we want them to develop true moral reasoning, not simply external compliance. In other words, we want them to choose to do the right thing, even when no one is watching.

Looking Beyond the Behavior

Parents drifting left tend to overlook bad behavior to keep the peace. Parents drifting right tend to focus on the behavior rather than considering the long-term goal.

For example, imagine that two students are caught cheating and the teacher contacts both sets of parents.

Parents moving left may respond as follows:

- "It happens. Haven't we all done something like that before?"

- "He's a good kid, though."
- "I'm sure he wasn't the only one. We heard your tests are too hard."
- "Can't he retake the test to make up points?"

Their first thought is to gloss things over and not make it a big deal. They think, "We'll get through this and move on." They do not give as much consideration to how the behavior and attitudes behind the behavior will affect their child long term.

Parents moving right may respond as follows:

- "Do you want me to cancel your phone forever?"
- "You're grounded, young lady!"
- "No field trip for you."
- "I hope you enjoy summer school while the rest of the family is on vacation."

Their first thought is to come down hard on the behavior rather than on the attitude behind the behavior. They think, "We'll deal with her and move on." They do not give as much consideration to how the behavior and the thinking behind the behavior will affect their child long term.

Veering Left Off the Road to Responsibility

Being permissive may feel like the kind and caring way to parent. Children who grow up with parents who normally veered left may develop habits that become easy exits. Often, they do not know how to take responsibility. These easy exits do not exist in the real world, so real trouble starts once they launch.

When Emotions Rule

When Mark and Jennifer attended therapy, they spent the beginning of the session explaining how their fifteen-year-old daughter, Erica, was a wonderful daughter. Then they added that, at times, she also was disrespectful and disobedient, treated her younger sister with disdain, was failing classes, and was hanging around unsavory friends.

The issue that finally pushed them over the edge was Erica's most recent problem. She had a job at a local convenience store and had been caught stealing. She was fired and was required to jump through a lot of hoops with the courts.

Jennifer complained that even though she was helping Erica with all her court requirements, her daughter was ungrateful and hateful and did not seem to show any remorse for stealing. Mark and Jennifer were looking for help and seeking to make changes, but rather than attending therapy along with her parents, Erica was on a ski trip with a group of friends.

These parents were drifting left. They had allowed their relationship with their daughter to be dominated by her emotions and reactions. When she was young and defied their limits, they would shift between lowering their expectations or yelling and becoming emotionally out of control. Neither approach changed anything. Erica learned that all she had to do was wait out their emotional blow up and go back to what she wanted to do.

When the therapist suggested they redefine their boundaries by taking away the new car they had allowed Erica to drive and, in its place, having her drive Jennifer's old car, Jennifer began to cry. "But she will be embarrassed to drive my old car. She really likes the new one. She'll get angry, and besides, I don't mind driving the old car. It doesn't bother me," she said.

Jennifer and Mark loved their daughter. They could not understand why she was being so difficult. They had tried so hard to help her and bent over backwards to give her a good life.

Somehow, they thought that if Erica came to therapy, the therapist would "fix her" for them. Instead, they were told that they had the most important influence in Erica's life— not a therapist, teacher, or mentor. If they would change, she would change. They were told that it would not be easy, and they should expect great resistance in the beginning, but it would be worth it.

Mark and Jennifer were strong in providing their daughter with warmth and acceptance, but they were working harder at solving Erica's problems than she was. Erica was unaffected by the problems she was creating. When Jennifer tried to put rules into place, Erica pushed back. Jennifer thought if she could just reason with Erica, she could get her to behave. She thought if she said all the right things, Erica would fall into line. It did not work. It never works.

Erica had no practice at managing her strong emotions. Mark and Jennifer wanted to keep the peace, but the last thing this family had was peace.

Eventually, Erica was sent to a psychiatrist, diagnosed with depression, and prescribed several medications. Her parents were afraid to demand anything of her, because they feared doing so would deepen her depression. She continued living with her parents and later had a baby that Mark and Jennifer raised.

Exits Off the Road and Using the Give 'em Five Conversation

One of the greatest difficulties parents face is not knowing what to do in challenging moments. They need skills and strategies that allow them to respond with calm confidence, rather than react out of frustration and anger.

Responsibility-Centered Parenting is a journey, not a race. It is not about external compliance, i.e. "making kids behave." That is a short-term, stop-gap goal. It is about our children learning to take responsibility.

Many other methods of discipline may come packaged with different names and terminologies. They may use any number of punishments or rewards, manipulation, or coercive techniques to try and get compliance; but at their core, the goal is the same: Get children to behave as fast as possible.

In contrast, Responsibility-Centered Parenting requires everyone—children and parents—to take responsibility for their own behaviors. However, they must first become familiar with the six common exits off the Road to Responsibility and the Give 'em Five conversation. These will be discussed in more detail later, but the following is an overview.

Closing the Six Common Exits

- Benefits for Changing Behavior
- Emotional Control
- Clear Expectations
- Consistency

- Leadership in Challenging Moments
- Response-Ability

An easy way to remember the exits is by using the mnemonic device "B-E-C-C-L-R: Be clear."

The centerpiece of RCP is Give 'em Five—an interpersonal communication framework used in challenging discipline scenarios. Learning to use Give 'em Five allows us to close the exits and keep our children on the Road to Responsibility.

Every conflict or confrontation will look different. No two scenarios will be exactly alike, because no two people are alike. However, the principles and process of Give 'em Five will remain constant.

As previously mentioned, the five components of a Give 'em Five conversation are:

- Support – Supportive comments given to and for the child
- Expectation – Clear expectations shared beforehand
- Breakdown – The Breakdown of those expectations, identified and shared with the child
- Benefit – Short- and long-term Benefits to the child, if they adhere to expectations
- Closure – Closure in the conversation, acknowledging next steps

*The six concepts and five components are capitalized to help readers learn and remember the key features of RCP and the Give 'em Five conversation.

The Most Important Responsibility Is Parental Responsibility

Before moving on from these concepts, it is important to recognize the issues of neglect and abuse. Even though personal responsibility is at the core of RCP, the most important responsibility is parental responsibility. It is always the parents' responsibility to provide an environment that is safe physically, emotionally, and psychologically. Abusive parenting does not find any place on the Road to Responsibility.

Parents who over-value control may go to the extreme of using corporal punishment to enforce the rules. They may even feel justified in being physically, emotionally, or verbally abusive. These parents will say it is for the child's own good. In highly controlling families, children have no voice. A child who is being abused in any of the forms mentioned above is the true victim.

Parents on the other end of the continuum may be easy going and have few boundaries and rules but, when taken to an extreme, their lack of order and attention may lead to neglect. They may fail to provide adequate meals, clothing, schedules, or boundaries for children. They may not provide safe supervision for children. Leaving children unsupervised can lead to physical injury, the crossing of sexual boundaries, or exposure to mature content through technology.

It is up to parents to protect their children from harm. The home must be, above all else, a safe place. Children are often the real victims in families. It is never a child's fault if he or she is victimized. No matter how out of control a child may become, parents never have a right to do harm to a child. When parents injure a child physically or emotionally, as a way to enforce the rules, this is abuse.

33

If you have found yourself reaching some of these extremes, remember you have the power to make the necessary changes. May you feel inspired to learn and use the tools we offer and give your children their best possible future. Please seek professional help and break the cycle. It is never too late to change.

Chapter 4
Clear Expectations and Family Foundations

If respect is a Family Foundation, then having a parent act and speak respectfully is as important as children being respectful of one another. With Responsibility-Centered Parenting, adults hold themselves to the same standards as they do their children.

RCP parents are willing to admit their mistakes. They can apologize and tolerate challenges from their children. At times, they even see respectful resistance as a sign of growing maturity and independence, which is the goal.

Family Foundations should begin with a statement, such as, "The Martinez Family will…" Below are several examples of possible Family Foundations:

We will support one another with our words and actions by:
- Attending one another's events with a supportive attitude.
- Lending a helping hand when needed, even without being asked.

We will treat each other with respect, even when we disagree:
- Speak to each other with respectful words and tone.
- Respect one another's opinions, even if they are different from our own.
- Respect one another's boundaries and things.

We will be honest and establish trust with each other:
- Tell the truth, even when it is difficult to do.
- Be truthful with others.

We will give best effort in all we do:
- Do every task to the best of our ability.
- Plan ahead to do the best job possible.

One's faith and personal family values may be incorporated into the Family Foundations. Keep the wording simple and age-appropriate. Revisit your Family Foundations over the years to update them and keep them age-appropriate.

Here's an example of a Family Foundation adapted for younger children:

We will treat each other with respect:
- Use kind words.
- Share toys and things.
- Ask before using someone else's things.
- Knock before entering someone else's room.

Our Parenting GPS

Because our brains lean toward fighting, fleeing, or freezing up during a conflict, establishing Family Foundations—

our Clear Expectations—helps keep parents focused, even in challenging moments. During challenging moments with children, parents can refer to the Foundations, which are written out and made visible. Foundations convey: "This is where we're headed." Without giving in or getting angry, parents can continue to remain on the Road to Responsibility.

Just as a Global Positioning System (GPS) helps us with navigation and orientation, establishing Family Foundations keeps us heading in the right direction.

Have you ever been driving in an unfamiliar city and lost your sense of direction? Without familiar landmarks, it is hard to trust our instincts. Should I turn right or left? Which way is north? How far are we, now?

If you have ever been lost at night while driving slowly, squinting your eyes, and looking for clues, you especially know the dreadful feeling of being vulnerable. Lost. What relief it is when you turn a corner and see the destination ahead! You regain your confidence, and off you go.

To reach our destination on the Road to Responsibility, we must turn on our parenting GPS. For RCP, Family Foundations provide this intentional sense of direction and constant guidance. When you are in the middle of a challenging moment, and you become tempted to lose your Emotional Control, you remember that your greater goal is to adhere to your Family Foundations.

For example, one Family Foundation might be: "Our family values treating one another with respect." Now, the focus is no longer on the inconvenience that triggered your emotions but on the goal of showing respect.

There is a time and place for offering choices, but parents who tend to swerve left undermine their leadership by continually opening new opportunities for children to exit off the Road to Responsibility. Offering age-appropriate choices for young children is the beginning step in teaching problem-solving in the Response-Ability process.

When parents negotiate with their children or explain in tedious detail why they are making new changes, they unintentionally give up their leadership role. Presenting the information in a brief and positive way is sufficient, but over-explaining expectations gives children the sense that you are selling an idea, rather than implementing a plan. And if you are selling, they may decide they are not buying.

Making an Investment of Time

Responsibility-Centered Parenting requires you to invest time in sharing your expectations at the front end of events and activities. Imagine if a boss were to lash out at you every time you did or did not do something they expected you to do, even though the expectations had not been shared or the task explained.

At times, this does happen with bosses, but when it happens on a regular basis, do we consider that person a good leader? Not likely.

When you refer to the expectations of a specific event, they will tie back to your Family Foundations.

Setting Clear Expectations will close exits off the Road to Responsibility.

Examples of common exits due to unclear Expectations:
- "But, you never told me!"
- "I didn't know!"
- "How was I supposed to know that?"

Examples of Clear Expectations that close exits:
- "Before we head to the grocery store, here are my expectations..."
- "Before our vacation begins, let's talk about our expectations for the trip..."
- "Before we give you the keys to the car, here's what we expect..."

Without Clear Expectations, children have no idea if they are hitting the target or not; and they will not be able to hit a target that they cannot see.

Demandingness and Responsiveness

Demandingness is a term that refers to a parent's ability to set Clear Expectations that are consistently reinforced. Parents who are strong in demandingness do not ignore bad behavior. They address it.

Responsiveness refers to how parents convey warmth and respect even in challenging moments. In other words, it is the ability of a parent to respond well when children fail to meet expectations, either because the children do not have the skills yet to meet the expectation or because they refuse to meet the expectation.

RCP parents have a balance of Responsiveness and Demandingness. They not only are thinking about the skills their children need today, but they are also thinking about what their children will need next year and in the future.

Permissive

When parents are under-demanding, they ignore behaviors they should address. They hope things will get bet-

41

ter with time. Rather than thinking, "What is the right thing to do?" children will ask themselves, "What do I want to do? My parents aren't going to do anything about it. They always get mad, but it will blow over soon." Parents in this category hesitate to set limits for fear of disrupting peace in the family. They believe it is easier just to ignore it.

Authoritarian

When parents are over-demanding, they value the rules over the relationship. Children may feel their value is based on performance and externals. Rather than thinking, "What is the right thing to do?" children will ask themselves, "How do I keep Mom and Dad happy with me?"

Effective Demandingness

Demandingness means more than requiring certain behaviors from our children. As you become more skilled in Responsibility-Centered Parenting, you will learn to:

- Set high but realistic goals for your child's development level.
- Communicate expectations early, clearly, and often.
- Teach, model, and allow for greater autonomy in accomplishing the task.
- Expect growing mastery over the task. It is a balance of teaching and trusting.
- Lead the challenging moment with your child and confront the behavior problems.
- Do not wait for a small problem to grow into a large one. Do not overlook bad behavior in a young child—

hoping the child will grow out of it. Understand the old adage, "Every problem was simple to solve when it was small."

• Have confidence in your ability to keep your child on the Road to Responsibility.

Some parents may insist on too much structure and control. If children are not given the freedom required to discover their own personalities, they may rely on others to tell them who they are.

Parents may set Clear Expectations but overlook the importance of providing the proper training along the way. They demand too much of a child without giving adequate positive Support.

The external structure parents set for the family, eventually, will be an internal construct for children. If there is little-to-no structure, children will have trouble managing their choices and directing their will when they are on their own.

Dad may say, "I expect you to keep up with oil changes on the truck if you want to drive it." However, if Dad has not taken the time to teach his child the steps necessary to change the oil, an exit off the Road to Responsibility could be left open.

Mom may say, "Look at this mess! Clean your room!" But to children that may mean, "Get everything off the floor." So, when the expectation is not clear, and young children shove everything under the bed to satisfy Mom, they may think the expectation has been met because their room looks okay to them.

Responsibility-Centered Parenting

Children do not feel supported and challenged in an environment where parents drive across the line, left or right. Our job is to help our children grow into self-sufficient adults who no longer need us in order to be emotionally and financially independent.

What is True Success?

Nearly all great stories center on a person or group of people who demonstrated strong character in the face of opposition. People who change the world for the better are always people of character. That is why movies like *Rudy*, *Miracle*, and *Glory Road* make us want to stand up and cheer. They inspire us to rise to the occasion and overcome great difficulties.

What is it about these movies that is so moving? It is a strength of character we see that keeps us rooting for the underdogs and celebrating when they overcome adversity. We are motivated by their strength, and we do not want to see them give up or compromise.

People who are remembered as being great are people of strong character. People who lie and cheat and who are selfish and arrogant may be well known, but their reputations will not stand the test of time. Make sure you define and model your family's understanding of true success.

'What's wrong with saying that word?'

Rather than having a thousand rules, Family Foundations establish a few core values.

For example, if a child says, "What's wrong with saying that word?" a parent may remind the child of the Foundation of "Respect" and say, "Our family is respectful of others, and that word does not show respect." A few broadly-written Foundations will keep the expectations clear, without having to rely on a long list of hair-splitting rules.

Where individuals have a natural resistance to rules, Foundations point the whole family to shared expectations which are noble, inspiring, and personally beneficial.

Rules assume a ruler.

> But when parents take the time to make the expectations clear, and then follow through with what it takes to complete the task properly, children thrive. Foundations provide a cooperative atmosphere that says, "We are in this together."

Foundations are a Priority:
Melissa's Story

Life experiences provide teachable moments and give us practical opportunities to keep our children on the Road to Responsibility. These lessons influence who our children will become.

It was toward the middle of my son Jack's sixth-grade year. He handed me an envelope with the word "invent" on the front. He rolled his eyes as he passed it over. Inside was a birthday party invitation from Denise, a classmate who was mentally challenged.

Jack and Denise had been going to school together since second grade. When they were younger, the other children were fairly kind to her, but in middle school life was not easy for Denise.

I asked Jack, "You're going to the party, aren't you?"

"I don't want to, Mom," he said.

"It might be fun," I said. "You can hang out with some of your friends…"

"None of my friends are invited," he interjected.

I let him know that we were not going to force him to go, but I acknowledged that he had been invited because he was kind to Denise. The kindness he had shown set him apart from other children.

"After all, Jack, our family values all people. Denise is just as valuable as anyone else." I told him how proud we were of him for receiving the invitation and I reiterated our Family Foundation of treating everyone with value: "It is better to be kind than to get an A or be a winning athlete."

Jack agreed that he would feel best about going to the party. As it turned out, we were out of town the weekend of the party, but Jack bought Denise a gift and gave it to her on the bus. This became a teachable moment and an important memory for him.

Our children are like wet concrete. These interactions make impressions that will one day be "set" as good or poor character.

Chapter 5
Consistency

Consistency builds a sense of stability and security in a child. Consistency is not about rules and regulations but about foundations of beliefs and actions that align with those beliefs.

When we establish beneficial guidelines—such as bedtimes and safety precautions—those expectations need to be kept with Consistency. Inconsistency opens a wide exit off the Road to Responsibility. A child can never feel completely confident when a parent's expectations shift and change depending on situations, moods, or a child's resistance.

Hardly anyone uses gambling or the lottery as their sole retirement plan. There are individuals who have made millions playing professional poker or picking winning Powerball numbers, so why don't more people turn gambling into a long-term retirement plan?

The answer is obvious: There is no Consistency. There is no sense of security that these activities will come through as hoped. It is the non-predictive nature of gambling that makes it so addictive—the randomness of a big payout. It may be exciting, but it is not stable.

Consistency Keeps Parents from Dispensing Random Payoffs

If people knew they were never going to win, they would not gamble. The small chance of reward keeps them going.

This has been demonstrated in experiments where some were rewarded every three times they attempted something. Others were rewarded intermittently (Skinner, B.F.).

The people who wanted to keep trying, and who were more likely to become addicted, were those who did not know when they would be rewarded. The first time, they were rewarded after four tries. Then they were not rewarded for twenty-three more tries. The anticipation, coupled with a sense that there was a payoff out there, kept them going.

We take our children to the grocery store and at the outset say, "I'm not buying candy, so don't ask." However, the last time we said that, they pestered us, and we gave in and bought them candy. In doing so, we encouraged the very thing we say we do not want: Having our children beg us to buy candy. We strengthened the behavior we did not want. We did it, not them. Our children were trained and incentivized to pester because *we* made the outcome a possibility.

Children are indulged by allowing emotional outbursts to go unabated or material possessions to go unappreciated. A sure sign that children have too much is when they do not value what they do have.

Children who are indulged may be denied opportunities to grow in areas of self-reliance, work ethic, persistence, and empathy. Characteristics of resilience and work ethic are more often found in families where children must put forth effort to achieve a goal.

Setting the Stage for Change

Setting the stage helps to prepare young brains to try something new. "In the past, I know you've gotten candy or gum, but we are going to do something new. From now on, you can earn candy or gum on every fourth trip to the store, if you can keep from asking. On every fourth trip to the store, you'll get to choose one piece of candy or gum."

Using this method places the focus on gaining self-control and not on getting things. This exercise can create a strength in a child's character that she can draw on in future struggles when she does not get what she wants. However, this approach can only be accomplished through consistency.

If consequences or rewards are dispensed with consistency, then it becomes predictable and dependable. This can serve to teach children the benefit of delayed gratification and builds self-control.

> There is something in us that becomes more motivated when we know that even though there is only a small chance that we will win, there is *still* a chance. When we are inconsistent, we create this sense of a random payoff for our children. With RCP, we understand inconsistency will only lead to more problems and create exits for our children.

Staying the course, regardless of complaining, pouting, or fit-throwing, will eventually end those unwanted behaviors. Giving in, even once, will prove to strengthen the behaviors we do not want. Instead, consistency helps with self-control and the ability to delay gratification.

51

Permissive

Issues of Consistency when parents drift left:

- No follow through on set rules
- Children leading the moment
- Parents passing the buck
- Feelings leading the moment
- Parents feeling emotionally overwhelmed by their children's demands
- Parents with too much tolerance for negotiation

What the Consistency exit may sound like:
- "That's not fair! You let me have a donut yesterday."
- "Why can't I go see the R-rated movie with my friends? I watched one with you last week."
- "Why does Jim (older brother) get to do it?"
- "Dad lets me do it. Why won't you?"

Authoritarian

Issues of Consistency when parents drift right:

- Consistency is often a strength
- Unwillingness to negotiate on anything
- Rigid rules that are inflexible
- Rules trump relationships
- Rules that do not evolve as children mature
- Parents enforcing the rules out of anger, fear, or frustration

What the Consistency exit may sound like:
- "Why does Mom get to act like that?"

- "If I said that, I'd get in trouble."
- "I'll just shut up. He doesn't listen anyway."

Establishing Clear Boundaries

Parents edging left may not establish clear boundaries. If they do, they do not follow up and require children to adhere to the standards. Parents edging right may have many rules, but they do not create a safe place for children to develop their skills. In both cases, there is a need for consistency to keep children on the Road to Responsibility.

Leadership When the Ship Is Sinking

Peter and Rebecca had never implemented a bedtime routine for their children, and they knew it needed to be done. They also knew that getting one started would not be easy. They were right. The children revolted!

The children had never been required to go to bed at a set time or even to sleep in their own beds. They had not learned how to soothe themselves to sleep. They only knew how to fall asleep listening to the television. Television had become their bedtime routine and, unfortunately, it had become somewhat of a surrogate parent.

At first, Peter and Rebecca could not see the harm in letting their children fall asleep in front of the television. It was easy. No resistance. Unfortunately, it was what they were not seeing—farther down the road—that would do the most damage.

Just ahead, over the hill and around the next bend—sooner than parents of young children can imagine—big children challenges would await. These challenges would carry on into young adulthood and life on their own.

If the parents' only goal was their own peace, they avoided short-term resistance. But when they realized they were not setting their children up for success, they saw things in a different light. With school starting and early schedules on the way, they decided to implement bedtime routines.

They had been so easy-going for so long, that the only way they knew how to do "something different" was to become harsh—overcorrect in their parenting, run off the Road to Responsibility, drive onto the shoulder, and bump, bump, bump along in the gravel.

They hated the feeling of being harsh with their children, but they thought that was their only alternative to being "too nice." Without a plan for staying on the road, these parents, and many like them, only knew two ways to go: Give in or get tough.

They told their children to go to bed and turn out the lights. Peter said, "If anyone gets out of bed, you will not be going to the pool party tomorrow."

The children cried. Rebecca cried. Peter went into the bedroom and watched the clock. Everyone was miserable.

Peter and Rebecca had made their expectations clear: "Get in bed, and stay in bed." They had given a heavy-duty consequence, because everyone was looking forward to the pool party. As Peter sat in his chair, the thought occurred to him: "What in the world will we threaten to take away tomorrow night … and the next … and the next?" Without realizing it, his questions were good ones.

Was this strategy any better than letting the children fall asleep where and when they wanted? At least with that plan, no one was crying. They were not sure which was more stressful—having a bedtime routine or not.

The following examples illustrate how different parenting styles may process this common problem.

Permissive
- "But they are so little. They shouldn't have to be so upset at bedtime."
- "I don't want them to grow up resenting me for being too strict."
- "I have to tell them all day to do things they don't want to do. I'm just too tired to do it at night."
- "What's the harm? They'll be fine falling asleep on the couch."
- "I'm so sick of being the bad guy here. I'll give in tonight and make them go to bed tomorrow night."
- "I've had a long day. I just don't have the energy to deal with this right now."

Authoritarian
- "You'll never be successful. You're so undisciplined!"
- "Go to bed now or no video games tomorrow."
- "When you fail class because you're tired at school, don't bother me about it."
- "I don't care how late your friends stay up. In this house, everyone goes to bed when we say."
- "When I was your age…"

Fortunately, they began to implement RCP, so they were no longer running off the road or overcorrecting. Instead, they were staying on course as a family.

They prepared for great resistance and challenging moments. They knew it would be tempting to fall back into their normal patterns, and their children would push hard. They reframed the children's resistance as a positive sign of change. They understood that resistance would mean they were making progress. With time and consistency, the children developed a bedtime routine that was not only a positive for Peter and Rebecca but also was in the best interest of the children.

Chapter 6
Benefits

Sharing Benefits for Changing Behavior can be powerful when the Benefits are shared as genuine, positive messages from the heart. For Benefits to be effective, they must communicate to the child that their parents are for them, never against them. We naturally tend to resist being controlled by someone. When we make a benefit about the other person, it removes the feeling and resistance they may have to "being controlled."

For a child to be able to receive the Benefits as genuine, the adult must have earned the right to speak into the child's life based on a proven track record of relationship rooted in unselfish love. This is part of the reason why many stepparents struggle with discipline if there is not a long-standing history rich with relationship. Much time and attention must be invested into the relationship first.

Most of us have experienced a correction or criticism from someone we did not believe to be in our corner. Did it help us listen better or make improvements? This is a critical issue that requires parents to take an internal inventory of their motivation.

RCP parents consider how a change will benefit the child, not themselves or the family.

Qualities such as respect, caring, and self-control should be highly valued by parents and children alike. The Foundations are not just for the children, but they also should apply to the entire family.

What a Difference

Most discipline methods set parents and children in adversarial roles with opposite objectives. With RCP, the shift in conversation from "Stop doing that!" to "You can do it!" is subtle but huge.

When you have been doing things one way for many years, it takes a lot of work to retrain your brain to think differently. Later, you will learn in greater detail how to utilize the Give 'em Five conversation in challenging moments with your child. One of the five components of the Give 'em Five conversation is sharing a Benefit. Some of the five components will come naturally for many. For most, the one that does not come naturally is thinking of a Benefit for the child. Ironically, it is one of the most important pieces of the conversation. The Benefit answers the questions: "Why should I do what you are asking me?" or "What's in it for me?" The Benefit helps children see how this will help them in their future or current situations.

Here are a few more tips on how to use Benefits to retain your joy, even in challenging moments:

- Remember what it was like when you were a child.
- Consider what you would want them to know.
- Share out of your wisdom and experience.

- Offer Benefits for the child, not yourself or the family.
- Share short-term and long-term Benefits.
- Make short-term and long-term Benefits age-appropriate.
- Connect Benefits to life and life skills, not token rewards.
- Connect Benefits to positive outcomes, not a fear of bad consequences.
- Personalize Benefits to the child as much as possible.

After you have established your Family Foundations, it is helpful to think through three or four age-appropriate benefits to help your child to master the foundations. The chart below shows possible Family Foundations, a brief description for each, and an explanation of how the Foundation may be used as a possible Benefit for Changing Behavior.

Foundation	Description	Benefits
Trust	Be honest	Gain more privileges
	Be reliable-do what you say you will do	Feel good about self
	Be loyal	Others will trust you
	Do what is right-even when no one is watching	Be given more opportunities
Respect	Follow the Golden Rule	Gain respect of others
	Use good manners	More opportunities
	Be considerate of other's feelings	Have more friends
	Deal with anger peacefully	Others proud of you
Responsibility	Do what you are supposed to do	Accomplish your goals
	Plan ahead	Be a good example
	Always do your best	Others can count on you
	Have self-discipline	
	Be accountable for words, actions and attitudes	
Caring/Kind	Play by the rules	Make a difference
	Share and take turns	Be a peacemaker
	Have compassion	Feel good about yourself
	Be generous to others	Have more friends
Courage	Stand up for what is right-even when it's not popular	Be a leader
	Persevere	Feel good about self
		Achieve difficult goals

Possible Benefits might include: making more friends, gaining respect, better performance, being more prepared for college, being a good leader, being safe, etc. Remember to keep the Benefits age-appropriate. Obviously, relating the Benefit to college would not be the best choice for a five-year-old.

If a child makes a disrespectful comment, a Benefit-oriented response could be: "When you use words like that, it's hard for others to hear what you're saying. But if you'll use more appropriate and respectful words, people may be more willing to help."

Bottom line: Benefits must be in the child's best interest.

Benefits for Changing Behavior stem from the Family Foundations:

- Character development
- Personal Benefits to the child
- Age-appropriateness
- Growth and maturity

A New Kind of Winning

Winning is not showing the child who is in charge. Winning is not proving you have the ultimate power. Winning is moving the conversation to a place where the child is more inclined to solve the problem.

> When the conversation is focused on Benefits, children do not feel like someone is trying to control them, so they may be more willing to work at solving their own problems.

Coming up with a Benefit takes practice, especially if you are accustomed to offering punishment and rewards. The first step is to replace the idea of a win-lose scenario with a win-win scenario for parents and children.

Benefits are about helping kids see their mistakes, take ownership of problems, and learn to do something different in the future.

Chapter 7
Emotional Control

One of the biggest challenges parents face in challenging moments is staying in control of their own emotions.

If a parent does not demonstrate Emotional Control, a child may exit off the Road to Responsibility by using these excuses: "Why should I be respectful, if Mom is disrespectful to me?" "Dad is a jerk. I should not have to be yelled at. I'm not stupid!"

Many of these attitudes and thoughts are never spoken. Nonetheless, they create resistance to the process of the child solving their own problems, and they turn the focus on the person who wronged them.

The problem with parents becoming angry is that nothing gets solved. And, after an angry outburst, parents may even feel worse because they have not demonstrated mature, Emotional Control.

When parents retain their Emotional Control, children can learn these skills as well.

{ Much like a calm lake where one can see their reflection, parents can provide a mirror for their children to see how they can and should respond in challenging moments. }

When we are impatient or sarcastic, it is easy for children to project that same behavior back on us. If we are mad or appear to be enjoying their pain, it makes us look bad and breaks down the parent-child relationship.

Lack of Emotional Control will look very different from person to person. A lack of Emotional Control is not about using a loud voice or shaking one's fist or using profanity. Some outbursts come in a passive-aggressive package.

We have all heard it said: "Be the adult. You are the parent!" So, why is it so hard to do this in the challenging moment? It is because we are human. This is why mastering the Give 'em Five conversation prepares us to respond based on our training and not on our emotions—much like paramedics are trained to act on their training rather than react based on their emotions.

Looking in the Mirror:
Melissa's Story

It was a typical morning, rushing around, getting children ready for school. My mood was unusually negative, feeling overwhelmed by the day ahead and frustrated with all the plate-spinning I had to do: packing lunches, looking for the permission slip I was supposed to send for the field trip (I swear I left it on the kitchen counter) and stressing about my 9:00 a.m. client I needed to confront about a tough issue.

With all this going on in my head, I snapped at my husband. My thoughts of frustration escalated:

"Why do I have to do everything around here?"

"Why do I always let that client get to me?"

"If I weren't so unorganized, I would have put the school paper in the backpack last night!"

Just before my husband left for work, he walked into the bedroom with a cup of hot coffee, handed it to me, kissed me on the cheek, and said sweetly, "I hope your day gets better."

Through the reflection of his kindness, I immediately saw my behavior clearly. I was no longer looking for fault in him as I had earlier.

Maintaining Emotional Control Even When Life Feels Out of Control

Not all parents are raising children in the most ideal circumstances. Difficulties, such as divorce or financial struggles, can add a layer of emotion to an already emotional situation. Parenting is not easy in the best of times, but for those facing hard times, there is always a temptation to "let children off the hook" or "come down hard."

As adults, we are called to step back from situations and deal with them thoughtfully, objectively, and proactively. In challenging moments, it is even more important for parents to use RCP.

It is important to remind ourselves why we should choose Responsibility-Centered Parenting rather than move off the Road to Responsibility.

No Matter How We Were Parented, We Can Become More Attuned

Attunement is a term used to describe what happens when an individual becomes emotionally and neurologically in tune or in harmony with another. Attunement happens when a person receives Support from another, feels validated, confronts a problem, provides a solution, and moves from a solution to resolution.

RCP and Give 'em Five support the process of creating and maintaining attunement. When we offer attunement, we are essentially saying, "I see you. I hear you. I relate to your internal experience. I genuinely care about you, and I am glad to be with you." Providing attunement allows someone who is struggling with Emotional Control to *borrow* self-control from another (who is attuned to them) until their own self-control is regained.

When we can offer attunement to another person, it is because our relational circuits are, in a matter of speaking, flipped on in the brain. One might describe this as having our heart open to another person. This is when we are genuinely interested in another person's problems and potential solutions. This opens our minds to think outside the box and explore new possibilities.

An Open Door

Attunement is like having a door available that opens into a room. In this room, people can connect at the heart level and find the freedom to solve problems creatively. When we open the door and enter the room—and the other person is willing to do the same—the relationship is strengthened.

The Give 'em Five conversation is like the door into the room. By choosing to use Give 'em Five rather than reverting to tokens or consequences, we step into a place of attunement and strengthen the relationship rather than damage it through indifference or harshness.

When we offer children attunement, we support them in the process of solving their own problems. The Give 'em Five conversation only works if we have attunement first— the position of heart and mind that is open to send the right message: "Even though we are having a problem, I am still in your corner."

When our children feel emotionally shut down or out of control, the mature RCP parent can share their own sense of calm with the child: "I believe you can fix this. How can I help you?" This invites the child into a safe place for problem-solving.

Relational Circuits

According to Dr. Karl Lehman, we are designed and wired for relationships. Even before birth, babies in the womb begin to respond to the sound of their mother's voice. From the time we are born, we look out into the world for a human connection.

When we are with someone we trust, and when we feel that others enjoy our company, our relational circuits flip on. This mutual response of connection strengthens the relationship.

ON
We ...
• See the best in others.
• Find others as a source of joy.
• Are glad to be around others.
• Are flexible.
• Are creative.
• Perceive others as allies even in difficult times.
• Can join with others in collaboration.
• Are curious about the perspective of others.
• Want to find solutions.
• Want our time together to be mutually satisfying.

OFF

We …

- Do not want to connect with others.
- Are suspicious and mistrustful.
- Are inflexible.
- Are closed off to the ideas of others.
- Cannot find good in the other person.
- Cannot recall past good memories about that person.
- Experience that person's presence as a source of irritation.
- Do not feel joy or expectancy.
- Do not care if the other person is happy or not.

Our children may show external compliance even when our relational circuits are turned off, but both parents and children must have their relational circuits turned on to resolve issues successfully and have closure in the conversation.

Flipping the Switch

Jan and Craig had been through the RCP training. They went home inspired and optimistic. Just when they thought they were making good changes in their parenting, they found out that their oldest son, Kale, had gone to a party where there was underage drinking.

Jan was angry, but Craig did not think it was a big deal. "Kale is eighteen. He's a good kid. Don't get so upset. I did the same thing at his age, and I'm okay."

Jan was angry and disappointed that Craig did not take her concerns seriously. She refused to talk to him about it. She had no tolerance for his input on the subject. Craig just retreated, knowing that Jan had shut him out as she always did when she was upset with him. "Why even try?" he thought.

Jan's relational circuits were off. She rehearsed in her mind all the many times Craig had not been supportive in the past. The more she thought about it, the less she even wanted to be in the same room with him.

Jan thought about their RCP training: "I knew it was too good to be true. I should have known that Craig wasn't going to change. That entire thing was a waste of time. We're never going to do this, because Craig is not going to get on board."

But while thinking about the training, Jan remembered what she had learned about relational circuits. She let herself consider whether her thinking had distorted her perception of the situation. She recalled a memory of Craig when he stood strong and held the line with Kale, even when she had not. Her heart began to soften, and she became open to the idea that she and Craig could solve this together.

Once Craig had some time to get alone and think, he realized he had been drifting left toward an exit off the Road to Responsibility. He struggled with confronting Kale, and he usually went the way of least resistance. He remembered what he had learned in RCP training. Kale needed strong leadership from his dad. Craig decided he wanted to provide this for Kale, rather than give up his leadership in challenging moments. Jan calmed down, Craig stepped up, and they both began to show leadership in challenging moments.

Chapter 8
Leadership in Challenging Moments

When parents are not sure what to say or do in a challenging moment, it is easy for them to revert to intimidation and lose Emotional Control. When we become angry or frustrated, we are not able to communicate as well. Instead of leading and communicating clearly, a parent may say, "Go to your room!" or say nothing at all—for fear of saying the wrong thing. For children, this offers another opportunity to exit off the Road to Responsibility: "She just sent me to my room for no reason." "He just grounded me, and I don't understand why."

If short-term obedience is the goal, then responding, "Go talk to your mom/dad…" or sending them to an aunt's or grandparent's house—or in the case of divorced parents, to the other parent's home—may seem like a good option. However, responses like this diminish the parent's leadership role when given on a regular basis. For children, it is an admission that the parent is not sure what to do and needs someone else to solve the problem.

Do Not Diminish Your Authority

When parents turn over their leadership to someone else, they may feel they are still in charge, but what children infer is: "You don't know what you're doing."

> At times, parents may look to teachers, schools, grandparents, or the other parent to "fix" the children. But by deferring to others, we are diminishing our leadership in challenging moments.

Leadership in Challenging Moments:
Angela's Story

I experienced the importance of leadership in challenging moments when our children were young, and I was teaching kindergarten. I would come home and face many of the same behavioral challenges with our own children that I faced at school. At times, I found myself saying, "Wait 'til your father gets home." I became frustrated because I felt our children listened to Larry more than me. By deferring to him, I was diminishing my leadership in challenging moments.

These unspoken messages diminish a parent's leadership role. Children will pick up on this abdication of authority and try to triangulate the situation. Therefore, everyone in the family needs to be trained and skilled to demonstrate leadership in challenging moments.

Why Challenging Moments are So Important

Most of the damage in the parent-child relationship occurs during challenging moments. Understanding and practicing RCP when things are going well prepares parents to demonstrate leadership in challenging moments and not to give up their leadership role.

Donna was not surprised when the school called with a concern about her daughter, Samantha. Lately, Samantha had been telling jokes and making comments that were not appropriate. Before she learned about RCP, Donna tended to drift left, then overcorrected and went too far right—depending on the day and how she felt at the time.

Permissive

Donna (to school administrator): "Do you have any programs at school that teach children not to talk like that? I can't get her to stop doing it. The other children laugh at her jokes, so it eggs her on. Can't you get the teacher to stop them from laughing when she does it? What about the school counselor? Can't someone there do something about it? You're the professionals!"

Authoritarian

Donna (to Samantha): "I just got off the phone with the school. Listen, young lady. If you're going to live in this house, you'll have to clean up your language right now. You're grounded. If I'd done that when I was your age, I'd have been tossed out on the street. I'm so tired of getting calls from your school. I keep my mouth shut at work. You need to do that at school. Do it or no more [phone, car, television …]."

Responsibility-Centered Parenting and Give 'em Five

Donna: "Samantha, you're a kind person and I don't think your intentions would be to offend others (Support). When you told that joke, maybe you were playing around with your buddies to make them laugh, but your teacher felt it was insensitive and disrespectful. (Breakdown) One of our Family Foundations is to treat others with respect (Expectation). Making a joke or hurting other's feelings is not worth the risk of your reputation (Benefit). Remember, a joke is only a joke when both people are laughing (Closure)."

An Attitude of Gratitude

Research identified by Dr. Dan Siegel demonstrates that the common characteristics of happy people are gratefulness, purpose, and self-control. If we want our children to become happy and fulfilled adults, we must model these characteristics and provide the structure and support they need to realize these long-term goals for themselves.

With the ability to maintain self-control, children are placed in the position to direct their own will. They have the freedom and internal strength to overcome adversity and press toward their goals and dreams.

When our goal is to close all the exits that lead children off the Road to Responsibility, we help them develop an internal strength that can launch them into more productive lives, even when we are not able to be right at their side.

In families where gratitude and appreciation are the norm, an atmosphere of love and acceptance is generated.

As parents, we provide the model for what it looks like to have an attitude of gratitude. RCP requires modeling gratitude and humility in front of our children. Offering children Support and Benefits asks us to find the good, even in difficult situations, so we are better equipped to lead in the challenging moments. The great thing is that when we make this a habit, we start noticing the good that has been there all along. We start to recognize the good around us that we used to miss, especially the good in our children. This makes the skill of providing Support and Benefits much easier.

All good character traits derive from a heart of gratitude and genuine appreciation. Just as a strong immune system requires good nutrition, a steady diet of gratitude and expressed appreciation strengthens our family's psychological system—its heart and mind.

When children can connect with what it feels like to be forgiving, kind, and generous, they get a taste for the great feeling that comes from making good choices. Then, that good feeling can be leveraged as a Benefit during the Give 'em Five conversation, with the Benefit being to keep having those good feelings.

Bottom line: It feels good to do good.

Staying Heart-Focused:
Melissa's Story

Kelsey was staying with me for the weekend while her mom and dad were out of town. I had several fun activities planned for us. Six-year-old Kelsey was a real joy—always a bundle of smiles and giggles. We made cookies, went to the park for several hours, and completed a few craft projects.

That evening, when Kelsey wanted to go outside to play, I told her no. She crossed her little arms, stomped her foot, and glared at me. "We don't get to do anything I want to do!" she said.

After giving myself a few minutes to think things through, I sat down on the sofa and invited her over to visit. "Kelsey, I am so glad your mom and dad asked me to take care of you, because I like spending time with you. We have done many fun things today (Support). It's good to be thankful for what we have, rather than only thinking about what we want that we don't have. Let's have you take a little time to think about the day, and see if you can come up with three things you were happy about doing. Come tell me as soon as you think of three things. Okay?" She nodded (Expectation/Breakdown).

After about five minutes, she shyly walked up and said, "I can think of two." "Great," I replied. "You're almost there. Just one more (Support). Go think of one more, and let me know when you have three things you're thankful for (Expectation)."

After a few minutes more, Kelsey was ready with her three things.

"Wonderful. So, what are the three things you are thankful for today, Kelsey?"

She rattled off many activities from the day. Her face lit up with a smile. "Now, Kelsey, put your hand on your heart, close your eyes and feel how that feels to think of the fun things you did today. How does it feel to be thankful?" "It feels good," she said. I asked, "Does it feel better than how you felt when you were upset about not going outside?" She nodded enthusiastically, and we went on to have a wonderful evening (Benefit/Closure).

Kelsey is not a bad child for seeing the glass half empty, but this habit would be detrimental to her future happiness. Had I said, "Oh, all right then, just go outside, if that's what you want!" or responded in frustration when she said, "We don't get to do anything I want to do!" the whole evening would have gone differently, and

Kelsey would have missed out on experiencing the power of gratitude.

Gratitude is a habit. The brain has a negativity bias. It naturally looks for what is wrong. With RCP, we look for the good. When we support our children, we recognize growth and individual strengths. The brain learns in short, repeated experiences. The Give 'em Five conversation helps parents and children develop healthy habits that are the foundation of happiness.

We can create an atmosphere where our children's hearts are open to our influence. With RCP, we are always communicating the concept that: "I'm for you. I'm in your corner." We do it not just with words but also with the tone of our voice, our facial expressions, and our body language. Children growing up in such an atmosphere will thrive emotionally and learn how to face their problems head on and solve them.

Chapter 9
Response-Ability

{
Response-Ability is the ability to respond well
even in challenging moments. When we solve
problems for children or only give punitive
consequences, children are free to exit off the road
and avoid responsibility.
}

By guiding children toward greater -*Ability*, we give them
time to solve their own problems, and we rely on them
to create real solutions.

If you still use time outs as a means for changing behavior
in your children, consider this: Is it developing a long-term
change in them?

Have you ever heard a teen who has finished two weeks
of being banned from a phone say, "Wow! Now, I understand why I shouldn't stay out all night without checking in.
Thanks, mom!" A seven-year-old almost never leaves time
out with a more positive, compliant attitude. In fact, it can
increase attitudes of defiance.

It would be wiser to do something that helps our children grow in understanding, responsibility, and internalized
self-regulation. As we say in RCD and RCP, "Unless chil-

dren are required to solve their problems, a time out simply trains them to *wait things out* rather than *work things out*.

{ Remember, anything that solves the problem for the child—including time, waiting it out, or removing a privilege—is not allowing your child to solve the problem. It is not time alone that solves problems, but it is how the child uses the time to solve the problem. }

Allow Children to Become Problem Solvers

We have parental responsibilities. Our children also have responsibilities appropriate to their age and ability, and they should be allowed to carry theirs—with parental encouragement and emotional support, of course.

When our children are little, there are countless responsibilities we perform to help these helpless little individuals grow into fully independent adults. Gradually, we shift carrying these responsibilities from ourselves to our children. Think of it as a backpack.

Parents' backpacks are filled with things like:

- Jobs or careers
- Household chores
- Family relationships
- Friendships
- Developing good character
- Personal growth and development

Our children's backpacks should get heavier as they mature. Five-year-olds' backpacks are filled with things like:

- Feeding the family pet everyday
- Choosing one's own clothes
- Getting dressed
- Learning to manage friendships at school
- School work

Teens' backpacks are filled with things like:

- Household chores
- Grades
- Friendships
- Driving
- Work schedule
- Time management

With RCP, the goal is to intentionally and continually allow our children to carry more in their backpacks in order to develop the skills necessary for independence. If we tend to veer left, we rescue children from the necessary struggle that will allow them to mature. Instead, we take their responsibilities on ourselves and weigh down our own backpacks—making their burden light and ours heavy. Children do not develop the necessary "muscle" that allows them to carry their load independently.

Exiting right makes their backpacks too heavy too soon. If we give them more responsibility than appropriate for their developmental age or if we emotionally disengage from them, we leave them without the support they need to grow in new skills. Children feel alone in their struggle—disconnected emotionally, but performing well in an attempt to feel appreciated, accepted, and loved. A child may become a human "doing" rather than a human "being."

If they are not supported well in the learning process, they do not get to make incremental improvements. When parents take a sink-or-swim approach to parenting, some children can become very discouraged and give up trying. Others can become "overachievers," trying to please, but because their emotional attachment is not secure, this creates other emotional, mental, and social problems down the road.

Both approaches—drifting left and right—have unintended consequences and allow children to exit off the Road to Responsibility.

Allow Children to Carry Their Own 'Backpacks'

Responsibility-Centered Parenting recognizes the importance of allowing children to carry their own age-appropriate responsibilities. All the while, parents are continually providing guidance and support as needed, but they are not solving their children's problems. Instead, they support them in solving their own problems. This allows them time and encouragement to grow in independence and self-confidence as they gain new skills over time.

RCP does not advocate "rescuing" children from their own responsibilities or overburdening them with responsibilities they are not prepared to carry.

A good rule of thumb is to look ahead a year and consider what skills a child will need down the road. For example, if a child will be entering kindergarten the following year, the skills needed might be tying their shoes, standing in line, following directions, or listening when others are speaking.

Rather than ignoring the requirements for these skills or demanding that the child "just do it" without providing adequate support, RCP parents invest the time and training necessary for their children to learn tasks at an age-appropriate pace. RCP parents allow children adequate time to tie their shoes before needing to walk out the door. Rather than getting frustrated, a RCP parent invests time in training and is willing to provide positive support.

This process continues even into young adulthood. If college is on the horizon, RCP parents prepare their children with adult lessons such as budgeting, laundry, and cooking. They turn over more responsibility for making appointments, hitting deadlines, and putting air in car tires. Rather than doing these things for their children or ridiculing them when they are ill-prepared, RCP parents expect the child to carry the responsibilities and provide training and support along the way.

London:
Larry's Story
When we have our first-born child, we are still learning, and they are our practice run at parenting. Many of the concepts embedded in RCD and RCP come from personal experiences, not only as a professional, but as a parent.

When my daughter, London, was very young, I was learning and developing my own thoughts and feelings regarding disciplining children. Like many parents, I attempted to use the traditional "time out." Along the way, I discovered the shortcomings of this popular method in trying to teach children right from wrong.

One time, I told London she needed to go to time out—just as the "experts" had said to do. I set the timer for one minute for every year old she was. London took her seat, which was a small wooden chair in the living room. I was in the next room preparing lunch. I heard noises and looked to see London playing with a toy. I told her to set the toy down. Once again, I heard noises and found her playing with items on the table next to her. I reminded London that this was not play time, but her time out. I moved her chair to the center of the room and went back to what I was doing.

A few minutes later, I saw London sitting in the chair with her head cocked back attempting to touch her tongue to her nose. When she noticed me watching she said, "Look, Daddy! I can still play with my tongue!"

At this moment, I realized just how strong a child's need for autonomy (the need to feel in control) really was. This is what began a stirring within me to come up with a method to teach self-regulation that would meet a child's need for more autonomy and not be focused on "time alone" to solve the problem.

What Are Response-Ability Mats?

Response-Ability Mats are a set of three colored mats used to help a child learn to self-regulate, reflect, generate solutions, articulate solutions, and implement his plan or solution. These are skills that will serve children well in relationships and life.

Red (Upset Feelings) Mat: This is the first mat a child may choose to go to if they are mad or upset. This is a safe place for them to begin to cool off.

Skill learned: *Emotional Control*

Yellow (Thinking) Mat: The second mat is a space for a child to begin processing what happened and what they could have done differently. This is where a child can begin to think of solutions to the problem.

Skill learned: *Reflection/Problem-Solving*

Blue (Ready) Mat: The last mat is intended to be an indicator to the adult that the child is ready to talk about what happened and share their solutions. This is where closure will be accomplished.

Skill learned: *Communication/Response-Ability*

The Response-Ability Mat process is sometimes confused with traditional time out, but the two are quite different:

Response-Ability Mats	Traditional Time Out
Child feels supported.	Child feels punished.
Child may choose to go or not.	Child is forced to go.
Child controls the time.	Adult controls time/set amount of time.
Child is actively engaged in process.	Child is passively engaged in process.
Child communicates (nonverbally) when ready.	Adult assumes the child is ready to talk.
Child is involved in a plan for change.	Adult implements change for the child.
Responsibility is placed on the child.	Responsibility is placed on the adult.

Remember, this process is *not* intended as a punishment or a consequence. We want to teach children a skill set they do not yet have. Using this as a consequence will deter them from using the mats as a tool to help them learn how to solve problems.

Once you have introduced the mats to your child, we suggest placing the mats in an area where you can easily see the child. Make sure the location has limited distractions (toys, TV, etc.). The mats could be left out if space allows or stored under furniture or on a shelf. The child could be responsible for getting them out and placing them in the designated space.

When the child is upset, he or she begins on the red mat. When ready, the child moves to the yellow mat to think about what happened and come up with age-appropriate solutions. Very young children will need some guidance at first. An example could be offering choices and then allowing the child to choose the option that will help him or her most. This also provides autonomy and increases motivation for change. When ready to speak with the adult about the problem and share solutions, the child moves to the blue mat to indicate that readiness.

When you see the child is sitting quietly on the blue mat, you speak to them about the behavior. We suggest using Give 'em Five:

1. Support – A statement of support for the child. Example: "I'm proud of you for using the mats to help you solve this problem."
2. Expectation – State the expected or more desirable behavior. These can be related to Family Foundations such as honesty, trust, respect, responsibility, etc.
3. Breakdown – State what the child was doing that was not meeting the expectation; i.e. not following directions, not putting things away, etc.
4. Benefit – Share a benefit of meeting the expectation.

This helps the child understand how and why it is in his or her best interest to change the behavior or meet the expectation. Example: "When you clean up when I ask you to, we can have more time to play later."

5. Closure – This is a statement or action that brings the conversation to a natural close, so you can move forward productively. Example: "Can I count on you to do this next time?" or "I know you can do this!" Closure could even end with a hug or a pat on the back.

When young children use the Response-Ability Mats, they are participating in a powerful process. Making the external to internal connection serves to strengthen their ability to slow their emotions and develop creative solutions. When introducing Response-Ability Mats, we recommend using the companion book we wrote called *Ricky Ritat Finds a Home: Teaching the Response-Ability Process to Children.*

Using Give 'em Five Improves Problem-Solving Skills

When children are supported in coming up with their own solutions, they are more willing to implement those solutions. This gives them a greater sense of autonomy and mastery.

Mom: "John, I saw you pinch Veronica (Breakdown). We have a family foundation of respect for one another (Expectation), and if she had pinched you, I'd be speaking with her about it. Most of the time, you and your sister get along, and you're a good brother (Support), but when you hurt her, that's not being a kind brother (Breakdown). You enjoy playing with Veronica, but if I can't trust you to be kind, you'll have to play by yourself."

John: "But, Mom, Veronica was calling me names. You didn't hear her."

Mom: "Okay, that's not respectful either, and I'll talk to Veronica about it, but right now we're talking about your choice to pinch her. What could you do besides something that hurts her? Take some time to think about it. I know, in the moment, you feel like doing something you know you shouldn't, but what are better ideas than hurting someone?"

John: "I could tell her to stop, and if she doesn't, I can go play downstairs. She likes playing with me."

Mom: "Those are great ideas. And you can always ask me to help if the two of you can't work it out. Now, let's talk about what you'd want someone to do if they pinched you…"

Throughout the conversation, Mom continues to close any exits John tries to use: "Why should I?" She shares the Benefits for Changing Behavior. She demonstrates Emotional Control, even if John loses his temper. She points to the Family Foundations, which provide Clear Expectations. She shows Consistency among all the siblings. She never diminishes her leadership role, but she shows leadership in challenging moments. All of this together reinforces the Response-Ability she has gained with continual practice using RCP and Give 'em Five.

Even if John's solution does not work the first time, the next conversation will focus on *why* his solution did not work, not on his original offense. Children feel empowered when they can solve their own problems rather than feel controlled when we "solve" their problems for them.

The process of thinking things through begins to build critical-thinking skills at an early age. It helps children learn how to have a good internal dialogue and build a good relationship with themselves.

Allow Yourself to Process

Psychological trauma is the result of a failure to fully process pain. Trauma may not have been life threatening, but children are young and vulnerable. Things adults may not perceive as threatening—harshness, shaming, neglect—can register in a child's psyche as traumatic.

Getting through life without painful experiences is impossible. Thankfully, new discoveries about the brain, heart, and mind offer us powerful tools for diminishing the effects of trauma on our lives and the lives of our children.

According to Dr. Karl Lehman, psychiatrist and neuroscientist, we must be able to maintain an emotional connection to another person in order to successfully process pain. Pain becomes trauma when we feel relationally alone, without help and support. If we stay connected, the result can be knowledge, skills, empathy, wisdom, and maturity. Using RCP and the Give 'em Five conversation, parents' strong leadership and emotional support during challenging moments create the perfect conditions to help children process life's challenges and learn to move past difficult situations without lasting emotional trauma.

A Beautiful Balance of Logic and Relationship

The right and left hemispheres of the brain have very different functions. The right hemisphere is the first to develop, beginning in utero, and it dominates our thinking for the first two years. It reads nonverbal cues, tone of voice, voice volume, and thinks in images. The left hemisphere comes online as language develops around the ages of two or three. At this time, children learn cause and effect. They learn to categorize and label things. When young children begin to ask, "Why?" repeatedly, their left hemisphere is hard at work.

As we learn to move back and forth between our right and left brain in our thinking, we can remain relationally connected and have true empathy for our children's challenges. We also can continue logically as we place the responsibility for solving their problems squarely on their own shoulders.

Having this emotional freedom to stay present and aware of what is going on in challenging moments, and walk alongside our children without losing our emotional control, is one of the best gifts we can give our children.

Chapter 10
Preparing to Use Give 'em Five

Whenever parents face challenging moments with their children, they can remain calm and confident because they know exactly what to do: Give 'em Five. Faced with any challenging moment, parents will master the following Give 'em Five tools to guide a child through the process:

1. Support
2. Expectation
3. Breakdown
4. Benefit
5. Closure

The tools remain the same, even though the order may vary. The parent's personality will make each conversation unique, while the structure of Give 'em Five will keep children moving forward toward responsibility by closing each exit along the way.

At the same time, the six essential concepts of RCP—Benefits for Changing Behavior, Emotional Control, Clear

Expectations, Consistency, Leadership in Challenging Moments, and Response-Ability—work together to keep children moving forward in taking responsibility.

Identifying Your Buttons

Before we can master Give 'em Five, we first need to address our emotional triggers. Most of us have not experienced the same level of trauma as veterans of war. Yet, the emotional process is the same whenever we feel threatened. Even in parenting, and even among the best parents, unresolved pain from our past affects how we deal with our children in challenging moments.

Add to this the challenges of today's fast-paced life and the lack of support systems of close neighbors and extended family, and all parents may, at times, find it difficult to stay calm and parent from a place of confidence.

Responsibility-Centered Parenting provides a structure to know what to do, even in challenging moments. To achieve this goal, it is important for parents to be honest about how situations in their past have helped or hindered them in becoming the parents they want to be.

The first step is to recognize that we have had experiences that were not ideal. We should neither suppress this reality nor allow those circumstances to define us or cause us to feel like victims.

Yes, we are affected by our past and current environments, but we do not have to be controlled by them. We do not need to assign blame to move forward and create a better future for ourselves and our children. We can learn from the past and choose to provide a safer and more secure environment for our own family.

A Cascade of Emotions

Many factors come into play when it comes to developing our Response-Ability. When we hear the term trauma, we may think of childhood abuse, violent assaults, or wartime experiences, but the brain and body do not have categories for different types of trauma. Any deeply painful experience, including shame, fear, rejection, and so on, may be registered by the brain as trauma.

When trauma is left unprocessed (not allowed to surface, be discussed, or be dealt with in a healthy manner), it can become a source of reactivity. Later, even a small, negative trigger can bring about a cascade of emotions.

The good news is that the brain has what is called "plasticity." The brain is quite capable of change and adaptation. Old, faulty thought patterns can be replaced with new, healthy ones.

Fortunately, individuals can rewrite their stories from an adult perspective and grow in their ability to respond rather than react. Writing a new life story requires us to find the good, recognizing the strength and courage that brought us through. This can be very difficult because there is a part of us that hangs on to the pain, sadness, anger, and injustice. This part does not want to be happy until things are made right.

Shifting perspectives from a child to an adult involves a higher brain function. We do not deny the pain, but we can learn to shift to our adult self. We can support the part of us that once had no voice, allowing our good story to dominate our thoughts and feelings. Over time, with repetition, this will cause our negative story to lose its power. "Even though my life had many challenges, I made it to this point, and I have what it takes to move on and grow." With the assistance of a capable therapist, new connections can be made and ingrained into the narrative of one's life.

Acknowledge Emotions

It is not necessary to dig up old memories or dissect every thought and feeling to step away from latent triggers. It does not take ten years of neuroscience to unpack the reactions we have that surprise and overwhelm us.

We can begin acknowledging the emotions when they start to surface. Neither ignore them nor give them undue attention. Just acknowledge them, let them surface, and feel the reality of whatever it is you feel.

By allowing yourself to process these emotions—sometimes in layers of understanding—you place yourself in a healthier position to parent your children through your own challenging moments without losing your Emotional Control.

Stuck in the Past

A young girl was in second grade when her family moved to a new state. The state she came from taught whole language versus phonics. The first day in the new school, she was asked to go to the board and circle the vowels in a sentence. She did not know anyone in the class, and she did not know what a vowel was. Everyone else knew what they were doing, but she was made to stand there embarrassed and ashamed.

Rather than redirecting the situation, the teacher said in front of the whole class, "Where did you come from? How could you not know something so basic?"

Little did she know that her one comment not only affected this young girl's feelings about the teacher for the remainder of the year, but it influenced how she would feel about the whole town.

Over time this memory faded, but it was still stored there as a memory—lingering just beneath the surface. From that point on, whenever there was a chance she was going to be asked to work at the board while others watched, she would be in such a state of anxiety that she could not access the information, even on subjects she knew. When the implicit memory was triggered, it affected her ability to think clearly, and she was drawn into a fight-flight-or-freeze mode.

Memories distort our thinking and throw us into a state of self-protection. Our brain says, "I will not let that (bad thing) happen to me again." An experience such as this, created by an unresolved trauma, results in us believing that we are not as smart or that we cannot work as quickly as others. We may not realize how it affects our ability to do other tasks, because our brains shut down from fear, not from a lack of intelligence.

This internal push to make sense of an unexplainable rise in our emotions can lead us through some unrealistic and unhealthy thought patterns. Quite often, these paths land us in a mindset of victimization and blame. We are convinced that our anger is because of the other person's behavior, not because of something that was triggered in us.

RCP and Give 'em Five Close the Exits

Imagine your child traveling on the Road to Responsibility. Each excuse represents an exit off the road. As parents, we want to close the exits. By using Give 'em Five, we can keep our children moving toward solutions.

Do any of these common exits (statements) sound familiar? "I didn't know."

"No one told me."

"I've done it before, and no one said anything."

"Other people were doing it, too."

Keep in mind that Give 'em Five does not guarantee that every situation will be redirected. The parent's goal is to close all the exits, so when children regain emotional control, their relational circuits are back on, and they are more willing to solve the problem.

It is common for children to look for exits from responsibility. When parents gain the skills of RCP, they will be able to identify and close the six exits in the moment, and use the Give 'em Five conversation to coach the child back on to the Road to Responsibility.

Exit Statements	Recognizing the Exits
"Why should I? What's in it for me?"	Benefits for Changing Behavior
"She yelled at me, too."	Emotional Control
"I didn't know."	Clear Expectations/ Family Foundations
"Mom/Dad let me do it yesterday."	Consistency
"Can I just go to Grandma's?"	Leadership in Challenging Moments
"Can't you just put me in time out?"	Response-Ability

Family Foundations and the Importance of Belonging

When we use Give 'em Five and the RCP approach, we always want to communicate how all our Family Foundations are intended to protect and honor everyone's opinions, possessions, and ideas. Throughout the Give 'em Five process, everyone in the family needs to feel they belong.

We need to be careful when we say to our children, "In

our family, we do this, or we do that." When we are not providing an environment rich in warmth and acceptance, the "In our family" approach can feel to a child as though it means, "If you don't adhere to our Foundations, you're out." For many children, this can foster a rebellious attitude: "Oh, yeah? Then, watch this!"

When parents drift left, children can feel they are accepted, but if the family's boundaries are too open, anyone can "belong" in the family—which is not always a good thing. For example, a mom may welcome strangers and acquaintances into the home to hang out or even stay a while. In some instances, children in the family may feel less valuable and, at times, be placed at risk of those coming and going in the home. They may feel less stable, because the family has no well-defined cohesion. When everyone "belongs" in the family, "belonging" loses its meaning and value.

When parents drift right, children can feel that "belonging" is based on performance. Children know what it takes to adhere to the family's rules to belong. This pressure usually backfires on parents when children become adolescents.

With Give 'em Five, belonging is a foundational pillar.

Heart of a Coach

Learning to coach and guide the Give 'em Five conversation takes skill, but with practice, the conversation will sound natural and genuine.

> Give 'em Five provides parents with a roadmap of where to go when their brains want to go to fight-flight-or-freeze mode.

Give 'em Five keeps parents calm and gives them confidence.

We like to use tennis as a word picture for the Give 'em Five process. Imagine a ball is the conversation. The parent's goal is not to win the match or to slam the ball back over the net. It is to interact in a positive way that benefits the child and keeps the volley or the conversation going back and forth while the child begins to solve the problem. Rather than approach the conversation with the child as an adversary or competitor, we want the parent to approach each conflict as a teachable moment.

The child slams the ball over the net. The parent volleys it back where the child can reach it. The child tries to slice it away to the corner. The parent sends it back with the same calm, consistent stroke.

Whenever things get tense, we recommend only two strokes, like a forehand and backhand, Support and Benefit.

When tensions mount, Give 'em Five allows parents to move back and forth between offering Support and sharing a Benefit until they can self-regulate and feel ready, willing, and able to clarify the Expectation, explain the Breakdown in the Expectation, and move toward Closure.

Although Give 'em Five may sound simple, it trains parents in profound skills as they learn to close the exits in the challenging moments and keep their children on the Road to Responsibility. As you become more skilled, Give 'em Five conversations will begin to sound less formal and more natural.

Support and Benefit, Support and Benefit

Like a tennis coach, no matter what the child "sends over

the net," the parent returns the ball with the heart of a coach, not a competitor. In challenging moments, the parent volleys the ball back, offering only Support and Benefit. This process helps provide attunement— when an individual becomes emotionally and neurologically in tune or in harmony with another. The parent continues using Give 'em Five until they reach Closure—where the child acknowledges the Breakdown and comes up with a plan to fix the problem.

Either through training or natural ability, some individuals seem better able to de-escalate other people's emotions. Others tend to escalate frustrations by "slamming the ball back" rather than "volleying it back" with Support and Benefit.

Mirror Neurons

The strength of modeling the behaviors we want to see in our children has been recognized for decades, but with the more recent discovery of mirror neurons, scientists (Ferrari & Rizzolatti) are uncovering just why parents' examples impact their children so powerfully.

Mirror neurons are a type of brain cell that responds when we perform an action or witness someone performing the same action. These neurons may be responsible for learning physical motor skills but, perhaps most importantly, they influence how children develop compassion and empathy. Mirror neurons allow us to feel the emotions of another person or mirror the actions of the other person.

Being in a family affords endless opportunities for mirroring. We watch a sad movie and cry. We watch a scary movie and our heart rate increases. We know these are just movies, but still we experience the emotions. To see mirror neurons in action, just observe spectators or coaches at a sporting event.

Recalculating:
Angela's Story

When we were first married, Larry was a wrestling coach. I remember watching him as he would coach one of his high school athletes during an intense match. Honestly, it was quite humorous. It was as if he thought he was actually wrestling, too. He would swing an elbow one way, then twist his body another, and he would motion as if he was maneuvering the opponent himself.

Clearly, he was not the one competing on the mat, yet it also was obvious that his mirror neurons were firing.

When parents can slow down their own reactions, they create the space to make a conscious choice either to mirror their child's emotions or provide the mirror for their child. They can make a choice to mirror the behaviors and emotions they wish their child to display. If we can slow things down and bring a sense of calm, while our children are feeling out of control, our children will have a better chance of slowing down their own defenses and opening up to our influence.

It is not always easy, but when we switch to Support and Benefit, it is as if our GPS says, "Recalculating. I will get you back on the right road to reach your destination." Focusing on Support and Benefit gives the stressed brain a safe place to go.

Model Responsibility

It is not unusual to walk away from a situation and wish we had handled our emotions better. Responsibility-Centered Parenting places personal responsibility as the top priority. The burden rests on us to model taking responsibility for our own behaviors.

Gaining a deeper understanding of what we are experiencing internally, when we are in fight-flight-or-freeze mode, can give us insight for making necessary changes. When we understand how we are being captured by our own thoughts, beliefs, and distortions, we are in a better position to take personal responsibility.

We cannot expect our developing, impulsive children to control their emotions when we are unable to stay calm ourselves. It is our role to coach them through their flaring emotions. When we are riding the emotional wave along with our children, things fall apart quickly.

Fortunately, challenging moments can strengthen our connections with our children. Imagine the lasting impact we will make in our children's lives when we use these times of high emotion as an opportunity to model self-control.

"Give 'em Five"
The Guided Conversation Checklist

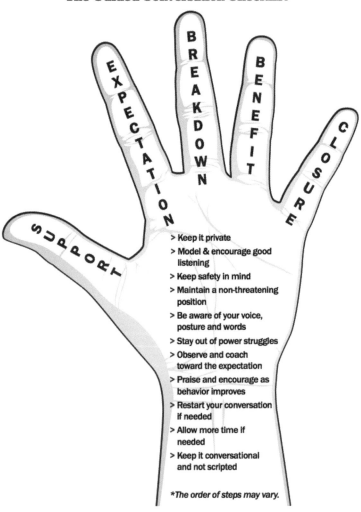

EXPECTATION

BREAKDOWN

BENEFIT

CLOSURE

SUPPORT

> Keep it private
> Model & encourage good listening
> Keep safety in mind
> Maintain a non-threatening position
> Be aware of your voice, posture and words
> Stay out of power struggles
> Observe and coach toward the expectation
> Praise and encourage as behavior improves
> Restart your conversation if needed
> Allow more time if needed
> Keep it conversational and not scripted

*The order of steps may vary.

Chapter 11
Using Give 'em Five

Offering a "high-five" is a commonly understood gesture of support. Therefore, it is a great metaphor for the Give 'em Five conversation. An actual high-five is not part of the conversation, but it illustrates the driving force behind Give 'em Five—a supportive message that conveys to the child, "I am for you. I want you to do well. I want only what is best for you."

Filters

Because Give 'em Five is less a static script and more an adaptive model for handling conflict in challenging moments, there is a learning curve for finding one's voice. To be effective and productive, Give 'em Five language must be personalized.

We suggest using what we call "filters" to judge whether your words and actions are appropriate. Everyone's filters may be a little different, but keep in mind our ultimate goal is for children to receive the message while continuing to keep their minds open and receptive to solving problems and taking responsibility.

Examples of filters:

- Imagine if the conversation showed up on social media.
- Consider if you traded places with your child. See it through her eyes.
- Ask yourself, "Would I talk to a friend like this?"

Support, Expectation, Breakdown, Benefit, and Closure

By now you are fairly familiar with Give 'em Five. In this chapter, we will go more in depth with each of the five basic components: Support, Expectation, Breakdown, Benefit, and Closure.

The components do not need to be used in a specific order. The more you use Give 'em Five, the more you will become skilled at making it your own.

Here is a brief review of Give 'em Five:

- Support – Supportive comments given to and for the child
- Expectation – Clear expectations shared beforehand
- Breakdown – The Breakdown of those expectations, identified and shared with the child
- Benefit – Short- and long-term Benefits to the child, if he or she adheres to expectations
- Closure – Closure in the conversation, acknowledging next steps

Remember the order may vary, but the final component of the conversation must be Closure.

Support

Showing Support for our children is different from offering empathy. We are not trying to prove that we know how they feel because they may not believe a parent can relate to them, and they may be right.

To be effective, Support must be relevant. Support also can be non-verbal and involve actions such as putting a gentle arm around a child's shoulder or sitting down next to her and listening. The non-verbal Support must relate to the relationship you have with the child and the role you play in the child's life—no more, no less. By considering some of the child's strengths, it becomes easier to be supportive in the tough moments as well.

Our Children's Biggest Supporters

Offering Support during Give 'em Five conversations is not a manipulative way to get our children to listen. It is not about flattery. It is about letting them know we are in their corner. Genuine Support comes from the heart. When we are looking for and recognizing small improvements in their behavior, we can be our children's biggest supporters.

Everyone is more open to correction when they feel understood. When we feel understood, it helps slow down our right-brain "bullet train" of reactionary behaviors. We can process better. We do not need to agree with our children's strong emotions, but we can recognize how they feel and help them learn what to do when they feel things deeply.

It only takes a moment to acknowledge and validate someone's negative feelings. What this does, in addition to calming the brain, is gives young children the vocabulary needed to share their feelings. Their minds begin to learn, "Oh, that's what sadness feels like. That is how it feels to be frustrated." *Name it to tame it* (Dr. Dan Siegel). When our children can identify their feelings, they can begin uncovering strategies on how to manage them.

When an emotion is strong, it can feel overpowering. Naming the feeling is a left-brain task. This helps to slow down the right brain that is immersed in reaction. Teaching children to name their feelings is not just a "touchy-feely" way to parent; it actually gives children a little time to slow down—like taking a breath—when the child's brain is over-focused on the problem.

Offering Support keeps us out of conflict mode and helps us continue to provide a calming and attuning environment for the child. Support says, at the heart level, "I see past your strong reactions, and I remember who you really are. If I remember who you are at your best, I can help you remember and, then, we can give you the time and space you need to solve the situation."

Be Your Own Biggest Supporter

If challenging moments with your children trigger your emotions, include a list of things you know are true about your child and yourself as well. "My daughter has a strong will, but so do I." "I love my son very much and want the best for him."

What are some positive truths about your child? What are some positive truths about you? Even though things may not feel good in challenging moments, when you are calm, you can turn your relational circuits back on by recalling good thoughts and positive memories.

Consider keeping a mental picture of your child that reminds you of the positives. Remember who your child is in the best moments, not just in challenging ones. "Even though I'm upset right now, the truth is that my brain is just trying to protect me. I don't need to fall for that trick. I can slow things down and remember who I am and stay in my leadership role."

What we choose to think about has tremendous power in our lives. It is up to us, as leaders of our homes, to take the initiative and get ourselves back into a positive relational mode. We remember our Foundations. We focus on the good in our children and think about possibilities, rather than magnifying the roadblocks.

As we do this on a regular basis, we are more likely to stay connected as we coach our children through the process of solving their own problems. This will keep us from trying to solve their problems for them. These repeated acts turn into brain habits that will become our default.

Here are a few basic steps to take when faced with difficult or painful situations:

- Be observant, and stay in a supportive role.
- Stay connected and in the present moment.
- Remain relationally open.
- Move your body into a natural, comfortable, and non-defensive position.
- Listen to understand, not to defend.

Expectations

Expectations should be shared with the child early and often. Posting the Family Foundations and Clear Expectations on the refrigerator or somewhere else in the home allows parents to refer to them whenever it is appropriate. This is a great way to keep everyone in the family on the same page.

When using Give 'em Five, parents can point out the expectation. For example:

Be Respectful...We will respect others' boundaries and property (Expectation).

"Ally, sneaking into your sister's room without asking isn't showing respect for her boundaries (Breakdown)."

It is not necessary to use the word Expectation, but parents should be clear and consistent about the behaviors they expect and the ones they will not tolerate.

When sharing expectations, it is best to state them in a manner that is not from a "top-down" control position. Anytime we begin a conversation with "I" it can feel controlling to someone who is already frustrated or angry. Examples include: "I already told you..." or "I expect..." Statements like these can invite more challenge and resistance. Some examples of removing the "I" statements would be:

"Being honest isn't just important in our family..."

"Part of giving your best effort means work before play"

"Helping one another is one of our Family Foundations."

By providing clear expectations, we close the exit statements we commonly hear, such as: "No one told me!" "But I didn't know!" "You didn't say I had to do it today!" or "It's clean enough."

Breakdown

During a Give 'em Five conversation, referring to a Breakdown of an Expectation should be a review and re-enforcement of a known Expectation. It should not be the first time the child becomes aware of a parent's standards.

Here's an example of using the Foundations to identify a Breakdown in the Expectation:

Tommy has not completed his homework before bedtime. His parents have made it clear that one of their Family's Foundations is to "Be Responsible" and an Expectation is that "We will give our best effort in all that we do." The Breakdown (not completing homework before bed) is what has caused Tommy not to meet the Expectation (giving his best effort).

Providing the Breakdown closes the exit of Clear Expectations and prevents us from hearing exit responses such as, "What? I don't even know what I did!" When we share the Breakdown of an Expectation, it is important to use details so that children know exactly where they need to improve and just what is expected of them in the future. Being clear and specific shows consideration for children, because it assumes the parent wants them to improve and is confident they can.

Benefit

Children can smell a phony comment a mile away, and no one enjoys being manipulated or controlled. This is why it is so important to offer Benefits based on what is in the best interest of the child, not the parents.

The younger the child, the more important it is to offer short-term Benefits versus long-term Benefits. As children get older, parents can share additional Benefits related to the family and the wider community, but it still should relate to how it helps the child.

When using Benefits with young children, it is important to keep the focus on things they understand and care about. Some examples may include: having friends, being safe, or learning new things.

Many younger children may be in an egocentric phase, so the Benefits must be age appropriate and directly related to the child.

The Benefit piece of the conversation is often the most difficult. Yet, Benefits keep the conversation on track and close exits. The Benefit for the child is to grow in the areas designated in the Family Foundations. When parents hear comments like the following, it may be an indicator that the child does not see the personal Benefit for Changing Behavior:

- "It doesn't matter to me."
- "I don't care."
- "Fine! I'll just do whatever makes you happy!"

Parental Influences on Moral Development

Dr. Grazyna Kochanska is a professor of developmental psychology at The University of Iowa. Her research on the development of the conscience—a sense of right and wrong—shows that children who experience feelings of guilt, sorrow, and empathy are beginning to develop a moral compass.

Parents who explain their parenting decisions to children as they go along, especially with a focus on the consequences of one's actions toward others, help further the development of more empathic children.

As children learn to recognize feelings of guilt, we encourage them—as we use Give 'em Five—to make the necessary repairs. This is when we see children begin to internalize the family's moral compass.

In those instances, we should not say to our children, "Don't feel badly about what you've done." Rather, we should say, "That's actually good that you feel badly about your choice. It says that you are growing. Thinking about how others feel will make you more kind and caring."

Having an internalized morality is the foundation of self-control. When parents talk with their children about feelings of guilt and empathy, it helps those children develop a strong, internal sense of morality. Because Give 'em Five always points back to the Family Foundations, it is the perfect tool for keeping the focus on character development.

In contrast, further studies by Kochanska show that parents who intentionally pile on shame and guilt curtail the process of internalizing a moral compass. We want our children to identify their feelings of sorrow and guilt, but we do not want to shame them. We want them to recognize how to avoid those negative feelings by making good choices, but we should never use shame in our Give 'em Five conversation.

Instead, we want our children to consider how someone else feels. "Did you see her face when you said that? Did you catch that sad look in her eyes? Can you imagine how she was feeling in that moment? What could you say or do to make things right again between the two of you?" We should let our children know we can all behave in ways we regret, but we also can work to repair the relationship and make things right again.

Forced apologies do little to build genuine empathy. Parents are not helping their children stay on the Road to Responsibility by saying things such as, "Tell your sister you're sorry!" The only lesson learned is that saying something is the same as meaning it, which is not true. This is another reason why parents must be genuine when using the Give 'em Five conversation.

Remind yourself that your goal for your children is not external compliance. The goal is internal responsibility and healthy social, emotional, and mental development.

Closure

Closure means the conversation has reached a point where the parent and child can move forward productively. If closure is not possible in the moment, it may mean the child has escalated to a higher intensity level and additional Support and Benefits are needed.

Closure does not mean children are in full agreement, but it does mean they are willing to accept input and put the issue behind them. Do not expect everything to be worked out perfectly. As long as there is movement forward, Closure is possible.

The following is an example:

> "James, I realize you may feel like your brother was part of the problem, too, and I will talk to him also, but can I count on you to do your part to solve this problem?" James nods his head in agreement (Closure).

Do not leave the Give 'em Five Conversation until Closure has occurred. A parent may have to tell a child he needs to put the issue aside until there is a more appropriate time to wrap up the conversation. The child may require some time before she is able to regain enough self-control to reach closure with you in the conversation.

Even though Give 'em Five is not a word-for-word script, it is a framework parents can follow in challenging moments with their children or even colleagues. The words individuals use will be different from parent to parent, but the components and process will remain the same.

Recognizing the Exits

Parents who have become skilled at using the Give 'em Five conversation begin to recognize which exit a child may be attempting to use. They have the skills to close all the exits through the use of Give 'em Five. If all six of the essentials of RCP (Benefits for Changing Behavior, Emotional Control, Clear Expectations, Consistency, Leadership in Challenging Moments, and Response-Ability) are in place, it will be more difficult for children to exit off the Road to Responsibility.

Retrain Your Brain

Imagine trying to solve an algebra problem versus recalling the lyrics of an old song from high school. The brain system used for the algebra problem—left-brain thinking—is slow and requires focus. The brain system used for the song lyrics—right-brain thinking—is quick and effortless.

You may wonder what this has to do with parenting. The answer is: Everything!

{ When parents become skilled at Using Give 'em Five conversation, they can stay calm, even in challenging moments. They can stay connected, and even joyful, because they begin to view challenging moments as teachable moments. }

It takes practice, but we can train our brains to move between left- and right-brain thinking. We can learn to create a harmonious dance between the two—using problem-solving to be creative in our responses. Even if it comes harder to some parents than others, this is a skill that everyone can learn and practice. Learning a new skill can be frustrating because initially it is all left-brain information. With repetition and experience, it will become your default. You can do it!

Unlike most parenting methods, RCP gives parents practical processes to practice until it becomes natural and even effortless to respond well. Just as easily as those song lyrics flow back into our minds, with practice, our RCP responses will begin to flow in as well.

When the two hemispheres collaborate, sometimes we describe this as "firing on all cylinders." With this, we are making the most of our brain's abilities. Having the ability to access both the right and left hemispheres will keep us from edging left or right off the Road to Responsibility. It gives us the ability to stay on the Road to Responsibility and provide a safe, secure balance between the mind and heart.

Encouraging a Joy-Based Home

All three of the Foster children—Megan, ten; Katie, eight; and James, six—had the responsibility of cleaning the bathroom they shared. They always argued about whose week it was to clean and what was required to finish the job.

Permissive

Bill and Janice were getting so tired of hearing the same arguments week after week. So much effort went into arguing that, most weeks, the cleaning was left undone or was only partially completed.

Every week was a slight variation on the same theme.

Janice: "Whose turn is it to clean this week?"

118

Katie: "I did it for Megan last week because she was at camp."

Megan: "I was at camp two weeks ago, not last week."

Katie: "At least you got to go to camp. You get to do everything,"

Because guests were coming over shortly, Janice stepped in to referee. Katie's comment, "You get to do everything…" stirred up doubts about Janice's own shortcomings and issues of fairness. She would move from sadness to frustration to anger. With the clock ticking and company on the way, she snapped: "Fine, I'll just do it myself."

From the children's point of view, this was mission accomplished.

Janice's tendency to veer left opened the exit off the road, because she did not provide Consistency. Also, it reinforced the children's sense that there was a payoff to arguing with each other.

Whether children do this consciously or subconsciously, they sense whenever there is an exit available off the Road to Responsibility, and they take it. Guilt, frustration, and indecision in challenging moments are some of the biggest exit ramps parents give their children.

Because she did not have a plan, Janice gave her children an out from their responsibility by not being consistent and clear with her expectations. After a long day at work, it was easier for her to do the job herself than to deal with an argument. As a parent who tended to veer left, the last thing Janice wanted was confrontation.

Rather than seeing her children as having the problem (a responsibility to clean the bathroom without getting upset), she took on the problem (cleaning the bathroom).

When we work harder at solving our children's problems than they do, we allow them to exit off the Road to Responsibility. We may feel we have solved the problem (the bathroom is clean), but we don't have a resolution to the underlying problem of the children shirking their responsibility.

Authoritarian

Bill and Janice established a schedule for the children. Bill monitored who was cleaning each week and stayed on them.

Bill [yelling]: "Megan, it's your turn this week. Get it done right now!"

He was tired of seeing Janice stressed and giving in to the children, but when he got involved, he would shout at them, which caused Janice to stress out even more.

Janice: "Don't yell at them!"

Bill: "Until that bathroom is cleaned, no one's using technology—bring me your phones! No one leaves this house until that bathroom is cleaned every day for the rest of the summer!"

Bill insists that Janice should be more in charge. "You need to keep track of the chores and remind the children. When they don't do it, you need to give them a consequence."

Janice tries for a few weeks, but eventually everyone slips back into their old ways. For all her follow up and insistence, the second she forgets to stay on them, everything goes back to "normal." The chores go undone and the cycle continues.

The children have not grown in their ability to work together or follow through on a project without being reminded, prodded, and threatened.

Nothing has changed except the day on the calendar.

Responsibility-Centered Parenting

Either Janice or Bill takes the time needed to show each child how to clean the bathroom properly. They talk the child through each step, slowly and positively, making expectations clear, so there is agreement about the standards and expectations. They ask the children to come up with a schedule that will ensure the task is done each week.

Katie is concerned about James. She says James will not do it when he is supposed to, and she fears she will get stuck cleaning it herself.

Janice recognizes this as a legitimate concern and takes James aside privately to discuss the schedule and go over the expectations.

Janice: "James, Katie is worried she'll get stuck cleaning the bathroom if you don't do it or you don't do it properly. She remembers times when she had to pick up the toys by herself (Breakdown). You are the youngest, but I know you can do a good job. I've seen you work hard in the yard when we have a project (Support). In our family, we work together (Expectation), and keeping the bathroom clean is one of those jobs that must be done. You three share the bathroom, so it is only fair for all of you to share the responsibility of cleaning it (Expectation). It's nice when you can go into a clean bathroom (Benefit), but that can only happen if everyone does a good job cleaning it on their week. Let me know your plan for remembering when it is your week to clean (Benefit). If there is still time this evening, you can come outside and join us, and we can have some fun together as a family (Closure)."

121

A Joyful Outcome

This did not eliminate the problem immediately. In the Foster's situation, it took time and intervention along the way, but with Janice and Bill's new skills in Leading in the Challenging Moment, eventually the three children developed new habits and could follow through on their chores on their own weeks. They knew there was no other option. Bill and Janice were on the same page. They were supportive, but they were also resolved.

At first, James did a poor job of cleaning and claimed he did not remember how. Yet, Bill and Janice did not give up on the goal—not the goal of a clean bathroom, but the goal of having James grow in responsibility, Response-Ability, and in his ability to self-initiate and follow through on a project.

All the children tried their best to get out of doing the work, but Bill and Janice remained calm, confident, and undeterred. They closed the exits by providing consistency and clear expectations. This kept the children on the Road to Responsibility and Bill and Janice from losing their joy as parents.

Ducky Duddle
Larry and Angela's Story

Do you ever find yourself working harder than your child is to solve their problems?

When our daughter, Lauren, was an infant, she developed an attachment to burp rags. She had to have her "Lovie" to sleep. She especially loved one with a picture of a duck in a puddle: Ducky Duddle. We tried to offer substitutes but, for Lauren, there were no substitutes.

It never seemed to fail. When it came time for Lauren to go to bed, Lovie was nowhere to be found. Parents of small children will relate to the desperation of hunting for the much-loved item, so they can get their child to sleep at a reasonable time.

We constantly found ourselves searching every corner of the house for Ducky Duddle Lovie. Night after night, we faced the same problem: Find Lovie! Our urgency was greater than Lauren's because we *wanted* to go to bed. She *didn't*.

At some point, we stopped and thought things through. Here were our options:

Permissive
We would have to add "keeping up with Ducky Duddle" to our already-long to-do lists. We would continue spending every evening turning the house upside down to avoid a screaming child at night and, consequently, an exhausted child in the morning.

Authoritarian
We would tell her, tonight, that *she* lost Lovie, so *she* would have to go without it. Then endure both her sobbing tonight and exhaustion in the morning.

Responsibility-Centered Parenting
Instead of veering left or right, we took an RCP approach. We sat our three-and-a-half-year-old down and told her that knowing where her things are would be important to her as she gets older (Benefit). We said we understood how important Lovie was to her (Support). We explained that leaving Lovie in different places around the house would make it

123

hard for her to know where her things were (Breakdown). Because she was so young, we suggested a solution, rather than asking her to come up with one on her own: She could choose a place in the house to return Lovie to when she was done with it (Clear Expectations).

Lauren chose to place Lovie in a basket next to the television. This gave us assurance that she understood the conversation, despite her young age. We continued to coach and remind her, but we also praised her when she remembered to return Lovie on her own. One day on a ride home she said, "Mommy, please remind me to put Lovie in the basket when we get home!" This is when we knew she was internalizing the information and taking ownership of the problem!

'Time to wake up!'

Many parents struggle with knowing what to do. For parents who have to do this alone, things can be even more challenging.

Every morning, Betsy called into her fifteen-year-old daughter's room: "Time to wake up!" Her daughter, Chelsea, would not budge. Then, at the last minute, she would throw herself out of bed, grab her gym bag and rush out the door—late again.

Permissive

Betsy: "Chelsea, it's 6 o'clock. Time to get up, if you want to be on time for practice." "Get up, Chelsea. You're going to be late." "It's 6:30! You're going to be late again."

Chelsea: "Where's my gym bag?"

Betsy: "I don't know. Did you leave it in the car?"

Chelsea: "If I'm late, I have to run laps. Help me find it!"

Betsy: "Here it is, under your jacket. I'll drive you, so you're not late."

Authoritarian

Betsy: "You're late, again, so you're not going to practice. You need to learn to be on time."

Chelsea: "Mom! I can't miss practice. If I do, I won't play in the game Saturday."

Betsy [yelling]: "You should have thought of that last night and gotten up when your alarm went off!"

Chelsea [yelling]: "But you didn't say anything about making me miss practice. I'd be on time if you helped me. This is so unfair!"

Responsibility-Centered Parenting

Betsy (to Chelsea Saturday morning): "Chelsea, in the past I have been wrong for waking you up for your 7 a.m. practice, rather than letting you set your alarm and wake yourself up. This hasn't helped you learn how to manage your time, which is a great skill for you to have. After all, you're going off to college in a few years (Benefit). I'm going to shift gears and be a better helper to you (Support). Starting Monday, I'm not going to wake you up (Expectation). I'm confident it won't take long, and you'll have this routine down. I know you can get up and be ready to go on time. From now on, you'll need to get ready on your own without me waking you up or helping you find your missing things (Expectation). Do you have any questions (Support)? I know you can do anything you set your mind to do!" (Closure).

Of course, Mom needs to be prepared Monday morning for Chelsea to test her resolve. She needs to understand that

Chelsea may have to face consequences of laps or loss of a game until she can figure out how to get up and out on time. Responsibility-Centered Parenting takes more intentionality—more work at the front end—but it saves time and effort in the long run. More importantly, our children are better prepared as they launch out into the world, and that should be our goal.

Safety or Soda? Breaking Trust

Meredith is a single mom with an eleven-year-old son, Darrell. When Darrell leaves school to walk home, Meredith is still at work. She tells him to go straight to the apartment and stay there until she gets home.

One evening, she sees an empty soda bottle on the counter she knows they didn't have at the house that morning. She feels so many things at once—anger, fear, and sadness. As a single mom, she feels the added responsibility to deal with this properly, but she is not sure what that means.

Part of her wants to apologize: "I'm so sorry we have to live in a place where you can't go out after school. I wish things weren't like this, and I'm doing my best, but you deserve better."

Another part of her wants to lash out: "You lied to me. You said you'd come straight home, and you lied. You could have gotten killed over a soda."

Back and forth she goes and, depending on the day and how she feels at the time, she may veer left or right in a very short time.

Permissive

Meredith: "You know I don't want you going to the store

after school. It's not safe for you to go out. Don't do it again, okay?"

Authoritarian
Meredith: "Go to your room, and stay there. I'm going to put you in latch key!"

Responsibility-Centered Parenting
Meredith: "I see you got a soda from the store. You're a good kid (Support), so when I say, 'Don't go to the store after school' (Expectation), it's about where we live; it's not about you. Unfortunately, it's just not safe around here. We both wish it were different, and I'm working to change that (Support), but for now, having you come home right after school is a safety issue, and it's the best we can do (Support, Expectation). We also have a Family Foundation of trust, and when you break that trust, it means I must check up on you more. I know you don't like that either (Expectation, Breakdown). What can you do to make sure this doesn't happen again? Unless you have a plan that works, we'll need to arrange for latch key, and I can pick you up there after work (Expectation). I don't mind doing that, if it helps keep you safe (Support, Benefit). You understand that, right (Closure)?"

Darrell will know from experience that his mom does not make idle comments. They will have a discussion regarding the latch key option and whether that is the best alternative. If there is another Breakdown in the Expectation, Darrell knows that, without a solution that works for both of them, he will be enrolled in latch key until he can find a way to be trusted in this situation.

'It's so unfair!'

When middle school student, Bradley, comes home after school, he is clearly angry. Throwing down his backpack, he says to his mom: "Mr. Walker is a jerk. It's so unfair for him to test us on chapters he didn't say to study. But I showed him. I tore up the test and threw it at him."

Permissive

Parents swerving left overlook incidents and tell themselves it is someone else's responsibility: It's the school's, the teacher's, or another parent's responsibility to fix the children's problems. They may side with their child to win easy points as the "cool parents," when really, they are abdicating their responsibility and allowing their children to exit off the Road to Responsibility.

Mom: "I hate it when teachers do that! How did the other kids do? You've always gotten an A in history. I can't believe he gave you a D!"

Parents swerving left may sound something like:

- "That makes me mad, too."
- "Don't worry about it. You're smarter than they are."
- "Let's go get some ice cream and watch a movie to take your mind off it."

Authoritarian

Parents swerving right may address incidents, but do it in a way that is too harsh or does not acknowledge the child's frustration. The child only hears their displeasure. Some parents might march their son up to the school and shame him in the process. Despite their best intentions, their child might show external compliance, but it will not produce the internal change in thought and emotion or the right-brain training that's required for healthy, long-term development.

Bradley: "Mr. Walker is a jerk. It's so unfair for him to test us on chapters he didn't say to study."

Mom: "I don't care if he is a jerk. You got the D and now you're grounded. Deal with it."

Parents swerving right may sound something like:

- "Life's not always fair."
- "You're too sensitive. Get over it."
- "Don't be such a baby. There's nothing to be afraid of."
- "Stop crying or I'll give you something to cry about."

A note of caution: With young children, it helps when we encourage them to identify their emotions by saying things like, "I see you are frustrated" or "I know you are feeling disappointed." For an older child, however, this may come across as condescending.

Responsibility-Centered Parenting

RCP parents offer Support, which calms the brain and gives everyone room to think and breathe as feelings of stress and anxiety diminish. Have you ever been upset and had someone ask, "Why are you making such a big deal out of this? Just forget about it!" That only tends to make things worse.

Bradley: "Mr. Walker is a jerk. It's so unfair for him to test us on chapters he didn't say to study."

Mom: "I know that what happened made you angry. You're mad that you got a D on a test after studying for so long. Mr. Walker has always been a good teacher. He's even one of your favorites."

Bradley: "Well, not anymore. I showed him. I tore up my test and threw it at him."

Mom: "Right now, what's more important than your test is your behavior toward Mr. Walker. I'm glad you're being honest about what happened and what you did. You know how important the Foundation of respect is in our family."

Bradley: "Well, I think it was disrespectful for Mr. Walker to give us that test. He doesn't respect me, so I'm not going to respect him."

Mom: "Bradley, everyone gets angry and feels they've been treated unfairly at times. I'm confident you will do what it takes to repair this, so you can go back to Mr. Walker's class tomorrow with the feeling that you made things right. I'm wondering how Mr. Walker felt when you reacted the way you did. Did you see the look on his face? I'll bet he was surprised, probably shocked, you'd do that. There's no excuse for treating anyone with such disrespect. Once you've calmed down, let me know how you plan on repairing this situation."

Later that evening …

Bradley: "I guess I'm ready to talk about Mr. Walker and what I need to do."

Mom: "Great. What did you come up with?"

Bradley: "Could you take me to school early, before the busses get there, so I can go in and talk to him?"

Mom: "Not a problem. That's a great plan and a very mature response. Let me know what time you need us to leave to get you there early enough."

With RCP, we recognize and acknowledge negative feelings—anger, fear, shame, envy, etc. We do not deny our feelings. We face them honestly and respond appropriately. We help our children develop the internal strength they need to manage strong negative emotions. We provide validation of their feelings while requiring them to address those feelings in a responsible way. Validation doesn't require a five-hour conversation about a problem. Although, at times, separate from managing their behavior, children may need to talk things out.

It is hard to think well when we are frustrated. When no one acknowledges our frustration, hurt, or sense of injustice, we have a harder time letting go of our negative emotions. Rather than finding a solution to our situation, we remain stuck in our emotions.

Extending an offer of Support helps the other person consider creative solutions. If using "I" statements to offer Support, be sure they are used as a Benefit to the child, not as a Benefit to the parent. "I would be happy to work with you on that math problem (Support)." Not, "I need you to do your math homework."

Parents trained in RCP may sound something like:

- "I see you are really frustrated."
- "How are you feeling about it?"
- "I'll bet you were disappointed when that happened."
- "Was that hard when things didn't go as planned?"

Give 'em Four

Acquiring any new skill may be hard at first. In the process of learning a new skill, our skill level will be lower, and our anxiety level will be higher. As we practice and improve, we become more skilled and less anxious. Ultimately, our goal is for our skill level to be high and our anxiety to be low.

An excellent way to practice Give 'em Five, in order to fine-tune your skills, is to adapt Give 'em Five to Give 'em Four. Give 'em Four reinforces positive behaviors, prior to any Breakdown in Expectations. We use Give 'em Four when we recognize and acknowledge positive behaviors in our children. Using Give 'em Four, we are able to practice four components (Support, Expectation, Benefit, and Closure) more often.

When we see our children doing something we want to reinforce, such as emptying the dishwasher without being told, helping a younger sibling, or cleaning up a mess someone else in the family made, we can use four of the five components in Give 'em Five, minus Breakdown (since there is no Breakdown).

This is a positive, confidence-boosting way to practice because it is unlikely a child will challenge us as we share Support, Benefit, Expectation, or Closure. More importantly, the child will enjoy and appreciate the positive reinforcement and will be more likely to repeat the desirable behavior in the future.

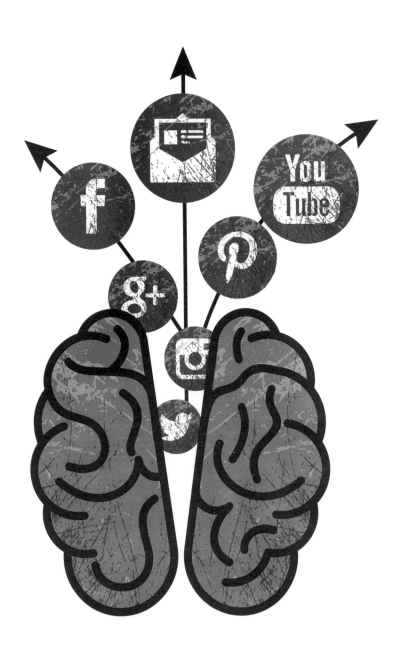

Chapter 12
Tackling Technology with RCP

Parents have concerns about the impact of technology on their children, even without knowing why. Little ones who constantly want to play games on their parents' phones and iPads or teens who isolate themselves in their rooms to play video games or scan social media represent a real challenge to healthy family relationships and social development.

What many parents worry about, intuitively, is backed up by neuroscience. Digital Dementia is a term coined by Manfred Spritzer, a neuroscientist. It refers to how overuse of digital technology results in the deterioration of cognitive abilities.

It only takes five weeks of digital use to see distinct changes in the brain (O'Gorman, *CTheory*). Areas of the brain responsible for planning, organizing, prioritizing, and empathetic-thinking atrophy significantly (Konrath, *Personality and Social Psychology Review*), as do the areas responsible for suppressing socially-unacceptable impulses. There is shrinking in areas of the brain that should, instead, be promoting empathy and compassion.

Sherry Turkle, the Abby Rockefeller Mauzé Professor of the Social Studies of Science and Technology at the Massachusetts Institute of Technology, found that those who texted more than one hundred times a day were thirty percent less likely to feel strongly that "leading an ethical life was important," compared with those who texted fifty times a day or less.

Sadly, the rise of technology is leading to a generation of shallow learners, unable to think deeply and draw conclusions from layers of understanding, perhaps unable to feel a high level of connection to others, even when they are in the same room. As a teen client once said in therapy, "I cannot feel my life."

Putting Technology in Its Place

Social media and reality TV have helped foster a narcissistic culture. It seems everyone wants to be famous, and this is very damaging to our children. In order to counteract these pressures, we do not need to give up our phones or take them away from our teens. We need countermeasures that require real conversations about real things.

We know that to feel empathy and compassion, the brain must slow down. The more distracted we are, the harder it is to attune to another person. The lure of technological distractions—particularly scanning (versus reading or thinking) and experiencing emotions vicariously through social media (rather than through real-life relationships)—jeopardizes family well-being. It is easier to hide behind various forms of social media, because these often make our lives look better than they are in real life. In the end, we feel more isolated from true connections.

When we create an idealized self in social media, we isolate our true selves even more. We not only disconnect from others, but we also disconnect from our real self and the issues we should be addressing.

Our submission to digital technology has led to an atrophying of human capacities like empathy and self-reflection. It is time to assert ourselves as parents, and put technology in its place!

{ It is through family relationships that children gain a sense of connectedness and a capacity to talk about their feelings. Our children need real connections, not the counterfeit "connections" they find in technology. When we talk to each other in person, face to face, eyeball to eyeball, something happens in our brains and emotions that can never happen digitally. }

This will never satisfy their basic human need for relationship. When we recognize the humanity in another person, and connect with them in a way that is true and transparent, greater empathy develops.

Bullies Love Anonymity

Bullies love anonymity. What you say in your car about the person who just pulled into your lane, you would be less likely to say to his face. Road rage escalates as a person thinks about how disrespected he or she feels. Self-control keeps these feelings from turning into poor decisions.

Self-control is about more than not doing the wrong thing. It is about controlling our thinking before we act. The less self-control we have, the more likely we are to make poor choices. Yet, we know that self-control is diminished through the overuse of "living online."

The opportunity to be distracted from our internal experience is always a temptation. It is easier to trigger good feelings by skimming social media than it is to get up and take a walk, but only one of those activities is healthy.

Technology Is Calling, but You Don't Have to Answer

Technology calls out to us. Can we resist the temptation to be distracted by email, text messages, social media, etc.? If you have concerns for your children, ask yourself what you are modeling. Are these distractions a big part of your life as well? If so, block out times for everyone to step away from the influence of technology and connect with one another.

Often, parents are as guilty as their children. Children desperately need parents who can model the proper place for technology. Intimacy requires our full attention, listening for more than surface information and reading between the lines. Being known and loved produces emotional intimacy, and listening with intention is a great place to start.

Parents provide the model for the self-control it takes to use technology in a helpful and responsible way, rather than using it in an addictive way. They have control over technology and do not allow technology to control them.

Rather than using technology in lieu of challenging family discussions, RCP uses Give 'em Five as a framework for discussion. We talk to each other face to face. We solve problems together, and we require our children to self-reflect and come up with their own solutions to their problems.

Families who settle problems through emails or texts may

say they do this to keep things from getting too heated. Yet, it is difficult to express true feelings, because our body language conveys the greatest amount of information; and, by avoiding conversations, family members are not practicing the skills they need to work through problems in a way where everyone is heard and valued.

Have we shown our children how to work through challenging moments while remaining real and vulnerable? It takes practice, and the family is the first and best place to gain this skill.

Parenting in a Digital Culture

Some parents may say, "Well, if you can't beat them, join them." They fear losing an opportunity to communicate with their children and being left out of the loop.

Children need their parents to be leaders, not peers. Having heartfelt conversations about our plans, feelings, and ideas will do much more to curb our children's appetite for false connections and negative peer pressure—especially online.

Studies show that even the presence of a phone on the table changes the conversation. People keep conversations shallow, since the phone may interrupt the discussion. It is easier to avoid relational intimacy and vulnerability, especially when we are not skilled at it.

Young people would rather text than talk. Phone calling is considered almost rude or inconsiderate.

In her book, *Reclaiming Conversation*, Sherry Turkle studied teens and found they would rather do just about anything than have a conversation. In a scenario where a close friend's father died, the teens said they would send a text, but they would not be comfortable calling their friend to offer condolences. The teens thought it would be too intrusive. The teens did not consider how their friend might feel if one of them showed up to be supportive in real life—not having to say a thing, but just being there. They had no frame of reference for the support and value this would give.

Technology Tips for RCP Families

- No screen time for children eighteen months or younger.
- Set clear expectations for both time and content on digital media.
- Give young children sensory-rich experiences (blocks, pots and pans, being outdoors, seeing, listening, smelling, and feeling), not digital experiences.
- If children are playing a game online, play with them and have a conversation about it.
- Unplug as a family and connect with each other.
- Find activities that encourage relationship, conversation, and laughter.
- Do not use media devices as a babysitter!
- Encourage "boredom," which allows for more self-reflection and creative thinking.
- Have a shut-off time for all devices (including the parents' devices).
- Encourage old-fashioned play (board games, cards).
- Get outdoors and away from all the distractions of technology.
- Sleep away from your phone.
- Work and study with the phone in another room.
- Turn off alerts.

- Schedule times you can check your phone.
- Set a good example by listening to children undistracted by any device.
- Invite friends over for an "unplugged" night of fun.

Olivia:
Larry and Angela's Story

Our daughter Olivia, who was fourteen at the time, was invited to an over-night birthday party of a close friend whose parents we knew and trusted.

We were so pleased when we received an email from her friend's mom letting all the parents know that if we needed to reach our daughter after 10 p.m. to please call her at the number provided, as they would be collecting all cell phones at that time to be placed upstairs.

It was no surprise to us when Olivia returned home the next morning full of stories of all the fun they had. We were happy to know that the parents of our daughter's friend understood how to put technology in its place.

Chapter 13
Joyful Parenting

Joy is a great indicator that our relational circuits are on. After a long day at work, do our eyes light up with joy when we see our child? We can see from the eyes of another person if they are glad to be with us. If we saw a brain scan in that moment, we would see that the right hemisphere of the brain was activated.

One idea for flipping on your family's relational circuits is to make a conscious effort to welcome each and every member of your family with a warm, sincere greeting that shows them you are genuinely glad to see them. Forming this habit will help bring and retain joy in your home.

Stay Thankful for the Small Stuff

Gratitude is important for moral development. Gratitude magnifies the positive in our lives and allows us to notice what is good, so we can experience joy in the present.

One way to develop a greater sense of gratitude is to practice being thankful and becoming aware of a feeling of thankfulness. That may sound strange, but in a world filled with negativity, we must choose to be intentional about keeping our hearts open to finding the good and magnifying it.

A fun way to practice gratitude as a family is to play *Four and One*. This game can be played at the dinner table, while riding in the car, or whenever family members are together. Everyone takes turns naming four positive things that happened in their day and one thing they wish they could change.

Be diligent to thank the people around you for what they do. Maybe you could start a "Thankful Thursdays" in your home. Encourage family members to tell another family member something they are thankful for about them by sending a note or text, calling them, or talking to them in person.

People who are consistently happy enjoy pleasure as it comes, but they do not feel the need to seek it out. Instead, happy people seek out connections and meaning. Happy people find joy in listening to and communicating with others. It takes intentionality to stay appreciative of everyday things, we find ourselves in a more content state where happiness and joy become our default mode.

The Power of Gratitude

Online banking is one of today's many conveniences. We can make deposits, transfer money, and pay bills all from our phones. At one time, that would not have been possible. Now, we take it for granted. Next time you use a convenience, challenge yourself to stop and acknowledge the benefit it has in your life.

Gratitude helps us celebrate our lives in the moment. It can make us feel more alive! It is like a blockade against negative emotions such as regret, depression, envy, and resentment.

New research on motivation and emotion from Dr. J.J. Froh, school psychologist, underscores the power of gratitude to:

• Reduce depression
• Make us more stress-resilient
• Reduce the length and depth of bouts of depression
• Reduce a reoccurrence of depression
• Block toxic emotions

We cannot have two opposing emotions at the exact same time. We cannot experience envy while, at the same time, experiencing gratefulness. During difficult situations, people who are grateful are more able to cope with their circumstances.

The Power of Joy

The brain loves joy and seeks it out. Newborns need to know that their caretakers find joy in them. Their faces light up when they see those they know. Being enjoyed by others is a basic human need. The people who mirror acceptance and joy back to us will have a great influence on our perception of our value and worth. We become the most like the people we have fun with and the people who enjoy us.

In RCP, we place a high value on joy. Joy has a deeper quality than happiness and is greater than our present circumstances.

{ Joy begins with having gratitude and finding the good in others, especially our children. }

Even when they are not acting like their best selves, parents can remember who their children really are and all they can be, rather than focus on what is going wrong.

RCP parents are also quick to observe and validate their children's progress in the process of character development. They also give them encouragement along the way—not just at the end of the effort.

We all like to be with people who enjoy us. Do you know someone who does not enjoy you—your personality, your ideas, your ways? Do you want to be with him or her? The people we are drawn to are people who genuinely enjoy us. Joy will sustain our families through the problems.

Our children long to be enjoyed by us. Our thoughts and feelings about them are of high priority. Even children who may put on a tough exterior and portray indifference to their parents' feelings do care that their parents value and find joy in who they really are. When we enjoy our children in their uniqueness—even through the difficult times—we can become a positive voice in their heads that they will hear their entire lives.

Joy in Challenging Moments

Mature parents create an environment where it is safe to have weaknesses. The family sticks together as they all learn and grow. Parents can be supportive to children while they work out their problems. They stay relational. They see vulnerability as an opportunity for connection and growth. Returning to joy after a challenging moment is imperative to the emotional health of the family.

When things get scary and they feel strong negative emotions, mature parents stay connected and find joy again together. Children learn that having good relationships does not mean there are no conflicts. Rather, good relationships will have conflicts, but joy-based parents will say, "I have what it takes to listen, connect, express myself, and work out problems."

'Unspoken' Rules

Parents drifting left may get drawn into their children's strong negative emotions. This tends to make children try to protect their parents from their true feelings. They think, "If my mom and dad can't tolerate these emotions, I will just keep things to myself."

Parents drifting right may struggle to be strong, calm, and self-controlled. They may be cut off from their own negative emotions, so they would rather not know about their child's feelings of sadness, fear, anger, envy, etc. They may make it feel emotionally unsafe for children to expose their own weaknesses. There is little tenderness toward weakness, so children wear a mask to cover their true selves.

Parents swerving left and right rely on unspoken rules to keep things going:

- "If you're upset with Mom or Dad, keep it to yourself."
- "Don't trust anyone outside the family."
- "Friends will betray you; only count on your family."
- "Little white lies are okay."
- "Wanting or needing something is selfish."
- "It's weak to show your sadness, disappointment, or hurt."
- "Always act like everything is okay, even if it's not."
- "Don't talk about anything meaningful."

- "No fighting. Conflict is not allowed."
- "Figure it out for yourself."
- "Don't notice the problems in the family."

Responsibility-Centered Parenting says, "We may not have the issue fully resolved, but we are okay now. We will allow our children to develop solutions, talk about their solutions, and give them the opportunity to try out their ideas. We are for them and want them to succeed, but in the end, it is up to them." Through their use of Give 'em Five, they communicate nonverbally that, "I am glad to be with you, even when we are having a problem. I won't reject you just because we have things to work out." The skills they model help their children know how to work out relationship issues and, ultimately, become better friends, spouses, and parents themselves.

Regaining Our Joy

So, what do we do when we recognize we are no longer joyful?

Here are a few suggestions:

- Listen to your internal dialogue and assess whether it is a mature voice that accepts responsibility, or it is a childlike voice stuck in blame.
- If is it a childlike voice, assess the age of the internal voice. Are you hearing very young language such as: "That's not fair." "Why do I have to do everything?" "You're not the boss of me!"
- Push back against your urge to shift responsibility to someone or something else.

- Commit yourself to using an adult internal dialogue.
- Stay present in the moment rather than running speculative dialogues.
- Speak to yourself as you would a best friend.
- Remind yourself you are a capable adult and you can improve the situation.
- Look for joy outside of yourself.
- Change the internal voice from self-blame and self-condemnation to: "Even though I'm struggling, I choose to love and accept myself. I will support myself as I grow and learn."

Helping Children Develop Positive Emotional Habits

Helping children develop a positive mindset and good heart habits prepares them to manage the inevitable bumps and scrapes of life. Qualities like humility, integrity, persistence, courage, and compassion derive from a foundation of gratitude. Emotions have a short shelf life. They are up and down. They come and go, but gratitude grounds children in the present so they can be happy and content right now.

Joy-Based Versus Fear-Based Parenting

When there are problems, RCP families do not panic. They act. RCP allows us to retrain our brains' default-systems from fight-flight-or-freeze to forming new right-brain habits.

An interesting finding about securely-attached two-year-old children is that they talk to themselves. They comfort themselves by talking to themselves out loud. They say the positive things they hear their parents say.

149

'Good job, London!':
Larry's Story

When my daughter, London, was about four years old, she loved to play outdoors. One Sunday morning before church, she begged to go out until it was time to leave. I told her she could, but I reminded her not to get dirty and that she needed to hurry to the car once she heard me whistle for her.

It came time to leave, and I whistled as I told her I would. She quickly ran and jumped in the backseat of the car, buckled her seatbelt, and then I heard her whisper to herself, "Good job, London!"

I smiled as I realized she no longer needed me to tell her when she had done a good job. She had her own sense of accomplishment. The message had become internalized.

We want to ensure that these internal messages our children speak to themselves are the correct messages they need to be sending, so they can be successful and grow in positive self-esteem.

We can use this same strategy. Rather than getting mad at ourselves when we blow it, we can be kind to ourselves, and say what we wish we could hear from a supportive parent:

- "Try again."
- "You'll get it next time!"
- "Don't give up."
- "You can do it!"
- "I believe in you."
- "It's about progress, not perfection."

Retraining our right-brain habits helps us turn off the

alarm bells, chase off the fear, overcome negative knee-jerk reactions, and get back into a positive relational mode. Then, we can problem-solve with our children rather than react to problems in a negative way.

Sadness and Anger

Sadness and anger are the two emotions that best indicate how a family copes with strong, upsetting feelings. Think about your own family. Which of these two emotions got the most positive or negative attention? Sadness or anger?

Was it safe to express sadness? Would someone help you? Were you told you were silly for being sad or too sensitive? Did sadness get you the attention you wanted? Was there a payoff in pouting or crying?

Was anger acceptable? Was anger seen as frightening and out of control, so it had to be hidden? Could children respectfully disagree with their parents? Could Mom and Dad express anger and frustration to each other in a respectful way? Did it take fits of rage to get anyone to listen? Did you get your way because of anger?

Remember, it is not just what we do in our relationships with our children that shapes their understanding of relationships. It also is how we interact with other adults. Our children are always watching and listening, taking on our attitudes and outlook on the world.

If we are often angry with neighbors, coworkers, our spouse, etc., children learn the world is unsafe and that they must live guarded. If the adults live in a chronic state of victimhood, complaining about how unfair life is and how they are mistreated and taken for granted, their children are shaped by these attitudes.

RCP parents can tolerate their children's sadness and anger without being drawn into the vortex of the emotion.

Our children can learn appropriate expressions of sadness and anger by watching our example. When these negative emotions are recognized and validated, then the responsibility for the expression of the emotion rests with the person who is feeling the feeling. There is no room for blaming others for our behaviors. We do not take away our support when our children struggle, but we let them know they have the power to tolerate negative emotions. They can learn to recover from sadness, disappointment, anger, and hurt; and they can learn from our positive examples.

Permissive

Parents moving left cannot tolerate their children's sadness. So, they rescue them rather than coach them to solve their own problems.

Authoritarian

Parents moving right cannot tolerate their children's anger. So, they get angry at them, rather than coaching them to solve their own problems.

Responsibility-Centered Parenting

Parents utilizing RCP do not reject sadness or anger. They remain strong and consistent in the face of expressed sadness or expressed anger. When using RCP:

- Do not try to stop the child's feelings by cheering her up.
- Communicate Support and respect.
- Communicate in a direct and clear manner.

- Coach him through the feelings of sadness and anger.
- Coach her on turning negative feelings into appropriate words.
- Coach the child on using her feelings to uncover and solve underlying problems.
- Ask questions rather than give answers.
- Ensure everyone in the family has a voice.
- Do not make alliances with children over the other parent.
- Value the unique differences in each family member.
- Forgive mistakes.
- See great value in the teachable moment and transformative, solution-finding process.

Being Intentional

Sam and Amanda had been married twenty-three years and had two sons, Jacob (age twenty) and Mark (age seventeen). The family was relationally connected and needed very little social service support, but to receive some of the agency's services, they had to be interviewed periodically by a mental health worker.

Their son, Mark, was diagnosed with autism early in his life. Now, he was in high school. He was driving and was even on a sports team at his rather large school. Mark planned on going to the local community college after graduation. It was clear that he had challenges, but he could function well, make eye contact, carry on a conversation with a stranger, and set some goals.

How did this couple raise a son with such challenges to be so independent? Amanda shared their journey. Both parents knew that Mark would, most likely, outlive them.

They would not be able to protect him from every problem. Therefore, they set out to raise their son to depend on himself and solve his own problems. They gave him every opportunity to have the chances their oldest son, Jacob, had.

With Mark's need for order and routine, they lovingly challenged his fear of change and coached him through the rough patches.

Sam shared an incident where Mark had become upset when the neighbors dug up a fence to replace it. Mark had buried action figures along the fence line, and now he could not find them. Sam went out that night with a flashlight and helped Mark look. They found most of them, but they did not find them all. Sam did not dismiss Mark's feelings. Instead Sam offered Support and coached him in coming up with options, now that some of his favorite action figures were gone.

This is a beautiful illustration of balancing demandingness and responsiveness. Mark's feelings were taken seriously, but they were not indulged. His parents provided coaching through challenging moments, but required him to come up with his own solutions. They were aware of his limitations, but they were always supportive while encouraging independence.

They also let him learn to drive, but they rode with him for a lot longer than they had with Jacob. They sent him to driving school, but they let him know it was up to the authorities to decide if he would get his license or not. He would have to pass the same test as everyone else. Now, he drives himself to and from school every day.

The warmth and love they had for their son was evident.

Had they driven too far left—never challenging him, living in fear of him being hurt physically or emotionally, because they did not want him to be sad—he would not have grown to reach his potential.

Had they driven too far right—becoming angry or harsh when he could not do things as quickly as his brother, yet not providing the necessary coaching—he would not have grown to reach his full potential.

Despite his challenges, they provided both demandingness and responsiveness. They allowed him to solve his own problems while providing Support. Their willingness to do the hard work early on made it possible for them to reap greater outcomes down the road.

Learning to Solve Their Own Problems

RCP helps us keep the long-term goal in mind. We need to be as proud of the solution and our children's effort to fix the problem than we were disappointed when they created the problem. Throughout the process, we use Give 'em Five to walk us through the challenging moment. When we feel we are not able to regulate our own self-control, we take a break, but we then come right back to the Give 'em Five conversation and pick things back up from there.

'You Can Be Proud of Me Now':
Larry's Story

As a single dad at the time, trying to potty-train my daughter, London, proved to be a challenge. I made frequent calls to my mom and sisters to ask for advice. I tried many of the typical "tricks" most parents try.

Although we were making progress, the occasional "accidents" were to be expected. I noticed that when they did, London would go off and hide. One day, when I couldn't find her, I suspected this to be the case.

As I peeked down into the playroom, I could see the wooden kitchen set that my father had built for her shaking. I opened the door.

"London, did you have an accident?" She nodded her head, affirming. I picked her up.

"Come on. Let's go get your pants changed." She looked at me and said, "Daddy, are you proud of me?"

"No, London. You have to tell Daddy when you have to go to the bathroom."

Holding up her thumb and index finger, she asked, "A little bit proud?"

"I love you, but no, honey! Not a little bit proud of you for having an accident."

I laid her down and gathered all the necessary supplies. Just as I did so, the phone rang.

"I'll be right back, London. Wait right here."

I took the brief call and as I turned around, there stood London in the doorway holding the wipes in one hand and the diaper in the other. Smiling proudly, she said, "Daddy, you can be proud of me now. I cleaned myself up!"

At that moment, something occurred to me that will forever stick with me. Children are going to make messes. When they do, we may not be even "a little bit proud" of them, but we can be proud of how they choose to "clean their messes up."

Our Wish for You

When it comes to the challenges children present, we all long for solutions. It is our sincere hope that Responsibility-Centered Parenting will be a long-term, life-changing, and joyful solution for you and your family.

References

Allen, P. Joseph and Land, Deborah (1999*) Attachment in Adolescence. Handbook of attachment theory, research and clinical applications.* Edited by Cassidy, Jude Shaver, Phillip R. The Guilford Press New York, London.

Baumrind, D. (1971). *Current pattern of parental authority.* Developmental psychology monographs, 4.

Berkowitz, M.W., and Grych, J.H. (1998) *Journal of Moral Education,* Volume 27, No. 3, pp. 371-1881.

Boyes, M.C. and Allan, S.G. (1993). Styles of child-interaction and moral reasoning in adolescence. Merrill-Palmer Quarterly, 39,551-570.

Carr, Nicholoas (2011) *The Shallows.*

Ferrari PF, Rizzolatti G. Mirror neuron research: the past and the future. Philosophical Transactions of the Royal Society B: Biological Sciences. 2014;369 (1644)

Fredrickson B., Losada, M. Positive Affect and the Complex Dynamics of Human Flourishing. *American Psychologist* (2005) October Vol 60 No. 7. 678-686.

Froh, J.J., Bono, G., and Emmons, R.A. (2010). *Being grateful is beyond good manners: Gratitude and motivation to contribute to society among early adolescents.* Motivation and Emotion, 34, 144-157.

Gottman, John M. (1999) *The Marriage Clinic*, W.W. Norton &Company, Inc.

Kochanska G. & Aksan. N. (2006). Children's Conscience and Self-Regulation Journal of Personality. *Journal of Personality*, 74:6 December.

Konrath, S., O'Brien E., Hsing, C. "Changes in Dispositional Empathy in American College Students over Time: A Meta-Analysis," *Personality and Social Psychology Review* 15, no. 2 (May 2011):180-98.

Lehman, Karl, M.D. (2014). *Outsmarting Yourself Catching Your Past Invading the Present and What to Do about It.* Second Edition This Joy! Books.

Lynch. S., Hurford, David P., Cole, Amy Kay. Adolescence 37.147 (Fall 2002): 527-49 *Parental enabling attitudes and locus of control of at-risk and honors students.*

Marsiglia, Cheryl S., Walczyk, Walter C. Buboltz, Diana S. Griffith-Ross, *Journal of Education and Human Development,* Volume 1, issue 1, 2007.

O'Gorman, Marcel. "Taking Care of Digital Dementia." (2015) *CTheory.*

Park, N., Peterson, C. Seligman M. (2004). *Strengths of Character and Well-Being. Journal of Social and Clinical Psychology*, Vol. 2, No. 5, 2004 pp. 603-619.

Ryan R. & Deci E. Intrinsic and Extrinsic Motivations: Classic Definitions and New Directions. *Contemporary Educational Psychology* 25, 54-67 (2000).

Schore, Allan, M., (1994) *Affect Regulation and the Origin of the Self: The Neurobiology of Emotional Development.* Lawrence Erlbaum Associates, Inc. Hillsdale, New Jersey.

Siegel, Daniel, M.D. (2011) *Mindsight the New Science of Personal Transformation.* Bantam Books.

Skinner, B.F. (1953) *The Science of Human Behavior*. The Macmillan Company.

Tangney J., Baumeister (2004) R., Boone. A. High Self-Control Predicts Good Adjustment, Less Pathology, Better Grades, and Interpersonal Success. *Journal of Personality*. Volume 72 Issue 2. p. 272-324.

Thompson, A. Ross, *Early Attachment and Later Development Handbook of attachment theory, research and clinical applications*. Edited by Cassidy, Jude Shaver, Phillip R. The Guilford Press New York, London.

Turkle, Sherry. *Reclaiming Conversation: The Power of Talk in a Digital Age* (2015) Penguin Books. New York.

Warner Marcus. Wilder J., *Rare Leadership: Four Uncommon Habits for Increasing Trust, Joy and Engagement in the People You Lead* (2016) Moody Publishing. Chicago.

Williams K.E., Ciarrochi, Heaven, P.C. (2012) 41:105301066. *Inflexible Parents, Inflexible Children: A 6 – Year Longitudinal Study of Parenting Style and Development of Psychological Flexibility in Adolescents*. Journal of Youth and Adolescence.

Resources

For additional books, Response-Ability Mats or other resources or for inquiries regarding training events on Responsibility-Centered Discipline or Responsibility-Centered Parenting:

866.865.1943

angela@givemfive.com

www.givemfive.com

About the Authors

Larry Thompson is the father of three daughters and a popular speaker and author in the field of education and leadership training. He has served in a wide variety of roles in education—from special education teacher to alternative and traditional high school principal. Larry is the creator of Responsibility-Centered Discipline, an internationally recognized educational program focused on creating more responsible children. His work has improved schools throughout North America. He is also the creator of Responsibility-Focused Leadership (RFL), and Responsibility-Centered Parenting (RCP).

Melissa Beck is the mother of two daughters and a son and is a Licensed Marriage and Family Therapist. Her ability to connect at the heart level with people from all walks of life has afforded her the joy of seeing many lives transformed. After years in private practice, she accepted a position as the Clinical Director of a nonprofit agency. Now, she is partnering with Responsibility-Centered Parenting to help even more families experience peace and joy in their homes.

Angela Thompson is the wife of Larry Thompson, the step-mother to his daughter, London, and the mother of their girls, Lauren and Olivia. Angela has over twenty years of experience in elementary education as a classroom teacher working with grades PreK through Grade Five. She is the co-author, along with her husband, Larry, of *Give 'em Five: A Five-Step Approach to Handling Challenging Moments with Children*. Angela brings her knowledge and passion of working with young children and the use of the Give 'em Five approach to working through the challenging moments with young children.